"My Heart Became Attached"

"My Heart Became Attached"

The Strange Journey of
John Walker Lindh

MARK KUKIS

Brassey's, Inc.
WASHINGTON, D.C.

Library of Congress Cataloging-in-Publication Data

Kukis, Mark, 1973-
   "My heart became attached" : the strange odyssey of John Walker Lindh
/ Mark Kukis. — 1st ed.
     p. cm.
   ISBN 1-57488-580-4 (cloth : alk. paper) — ISBN 1-57488-759-9 (pbk.:
alk. paper)
    1. Lindh, John Walker, 1981– 2. Terrorists—Biography. 3. Muslim
converts from Christianity—Biography. 4. Americans—Arab
countries—Biography. 5. Americans—Afghanistan—Biography. 6.
Taliban. 7. Jihad. I. Title.

HV6430.L55K85   2003
958.104'6—dc21   2003006954

Brassey's, Inc.
22841 Quicksilver Drive
Dulles, Virginia 20166

First Edition

10 9 8 7 6 5 4 3 2 1

For my mother, my father, Marinell, Heidi and Steve,
a family whose support made this writing
and so much else possible for me.

Contents

Acknowledgments

SOME of the most important research done for this book would have been impossible without Sajjad Tarakzai, a Pakistani journalist who risked his life on several occasions serving as my translator and guide in Pakistan. I am deeply grateful for the long hours of difficult, dangerous work he undertook to help me through many months, in which he proved to be both a skilled professional and trustworthy friend. My agent, Elizabeth Frost-Knappman of New England Publishing Associates, and my editor, Christina Davidson, provided support from half way around the world through many difficult months as well. And I owe special thanks to Alex Canizares, a friend who made traveling nearly as easy as coming home. Dozens more provided help in large and small ways throughout the writing of this book. Here are some, but by no means all: Erin Mewhirter, Richard Glick, Kim Zimmerman, Adam Gerson, Esther Oxford, Hedi Aouidj, Zarif Amiri, Asra Nomani, Kerry Lauerman, Thorne Anderson, Mohammed Saleem, Dan Olmsted, Shaun Waterman, Eli J. Lake, David Fechheimer, Barry Simon, Ebrahim Nana, Mohamed Sallam al-Asbahi, Karin Thayer, Abduh Moqbil Assabri, Robert Young Pelton, Gen. Rashid Dostum, Comdr. Mohamed Atta.

Author's Note

JOHN PHILLIP WALKER LINDH could not be interviewed for this book. At the time of writing, Lindh remained under special prison restrictions imposed by the Justice Department that prevent him from speaking directly or indirectly to the public, despite a plea agreement that left his case settled officially on October 4, 2002. His is the most important voice missing in this story, but others are missing too, unfortunately. Lindh's parents, Marilyn Walker and Frank Lindh, refused to be interviewed for this book, after having cooperated with a series of media outlets, which they felt ultimately treated them and their son unfairly. Many of Lindh's Muslim peers in California, Yemen, and Pakistan also declined, some for the same reason as Lindh's parents, others fearing risk to their reputations and personal safety if publicly tied to Lindh.

Easily the most disappointing absences, however, are the Taliban fighters and commanders who knew Lindh during his time in Afghanistan. They simply could not be found in the aftermath of the U.S. military campaign in Afghanistan, though I spent several months searching for them in Pakistan and Afghanistan during the early part of 2002, when I first began writing this book.

Lindh was captured by American forces on December 1, 2001, outside Mazar-i-Sharif, Afghanistan, after a savage battle at a prison fortress that he and other foreign fighters for the Taliban narrowly survived. At the time, I was elsewhere in Afghanistan covering other fighting as a freelance journalist, so I missed much of the media attention his story first generated. But in the weeks afterward, I found myself idling in Islamabad, Pakistan, hearing more about Lindh and becoming increasingly curious, along with millions of others who followed the story.

Before going into U.S. custody, Lindh spoke briefly with CNN. His one television appearance fueled months of media attention, making him a regular presence in newscasts, magazines, and newspapers, as well as online reports. With figures like Osama bin Laden and Taliban leader Mullah Mohammed Omar suddenly out of the picture at the war's close, Lindh for a time became the public face of September 11, a persona representing many different things to different people on all sides of a confusing conflict. In the United States, some labeled Lindh a traitor and talked about executing him. In Pakistan, where I was, Lindh was becoming something of a folk hero, a madrassa myth whom young jihadis saw as the ultimate validation for their cause. While Lindh remained locked up awaiting trial for most of 2002, his fame grew in strange ways, until eventually he emerged in global society as a champion and a pariah, the focus of hatred and sympathy, the butt of late-night jokes, the subject of a Steve Earle song, and the cause célèbre of an Internet site (www.freejohnwalker.net). Theories about his motivations — psychological, political, religious, and personal — swirled in the media and popular discourse, but offered little understanding. Personally, I found Lindh's story fascinating in all its improbable drama, without feeling much emotion about Lindh himself either way. And I vowed to keep an open mind when in the spring of 2002, backed by my publisher, I began retracing Lindh's steps through Pakistan and Afghanistan, seeking people to interview who either knew Lindh or witnessed events he experienced along the way. Eventually, I traveled to Yemen and the San Francisco area doing the same thing, with mixed success in each place.

"It will be difficult for you to find Suleyman's classmates," said Hamid, an arms instructor for the Pakistani Islamic militant group Harkat ul Mujaheddin, who knew Lindh by one of his aliases when he trained with the group before joining the Taliban. I found Hamid in Mansehra, a small town in the mountains of northern Pakistan. "Some of them are dispersed, and most of them have become martyrs."

Hamid, who himself had been difficult to locate, was right. Few of Lindh's comrades were around, and those who were, largely, felt reluctant to talk. Still, many who knew Lindh did come forward, people ranging from his earliest Muslim friends in California to Northern Alliance soldiers who fought against him and his foreign Taliban comrades in Afghanistan.

Lindh's lawyers, in particular, were a valuable source of information as the people who had spent the most time with him hearing his story. At times in these pages, I purport to know what Lindh might have been thinking or feeling. This writing is based on what I could piece together through the various public statements of James Brosnahan, George Harris, and Tony West, as well as my interviews with them.

Lindh's attorneys were among my last interview subjects when they sat with me in San Francisco in December of 2002. By then, I had lost count of how many people talked to me about Lindh. Somewhere in Afghanistan the number passed two hundred, with most of the individuals I found unable to offer a deeper understanding of Lindh or his travels and times than was commonly known. The few who could offer real insight appear by name in the coming pages. Also, as part of my research, I read in detail hundreds of pages of court documents filed in Lindh's case and pored over as many media accounts about him. What follows is the fullest, most in-depth chronicle to date of Lindh's saga.

Some have argued to me, with good reason, that Lindh is too

young and too insignificant to merit a biography. In part I agree, because in many ways I've found Lindh unremarkable. His teenage conversion to Islam, for example, was somewhat unusual, but nothing extraordinary. Many would argue that Lindh's adolescent spiritual transformation represented a troubled search for identity and a disturbing denouncement of his native culture that reflected issues in his upbringing. I don't see it that way. Lindh, like many young people, explored religion. He had enough curiosity to open himself to faiths largely outside the society of his birth, an admirable trait that speaks to his intellectual nature and underscores his implicit appreciation of religious freedoms in America. Lindh found meaning in Islam, as do more than one billion people worldwide, including around eight million in the United States — hardly a unique occurrence. Once Lindh adopted Islam, he practiced the religion with a committed convert's earnestness. Many Islamic neophytes lean toward a liberal interpretation of the religion that lends itself to Islamic orthodoxy and conservatism.

What sets Lindh apart from other Americans and other Muslims is the course he chose for himself after his religious conversion. Lindh's early choice to become a Muslim without doubt profoundly altered his life, but it wasn't the choice that put him where he is today, jailed in a federal prison, occupying a corner of our minds as a figure linked to September 11. Therefore, in these pages I've focused mainly on Lindh's journeys, rather than his upbringing and initial religious exploration, for the unusual steps he took in Yemen, Pakistan, and Afghanistan are what make his story unique. Untold millions have adopted Islam in recent years in the United States and across the globe. Only a handful of those converts wound up fighting in Afghanistan. And still fewer who fought there hailed from the United States. But again, Lindh is not as unusual as he might seem, given the history, albeit little-known, of other Americans who have taken a similar path to Afghanistan and Muslim conflict zones elsewhere on the planet.

One aspect I found most surprising about Lindh's story was how easily someone of his admitted ignorance moved through such disparate worlds. Here was a young man with a high-school education and no experience traveling abroad who managed to join the company of Osama bin Laden not once, but several times, before soldiering in Afghanistan. Part of the explanation for why and how he did so comes from recent decades of American policy towards the Islamic world. For instance, Lindh's first inklings about jihad in Afghanistan came largely from Yemenis who had fought there in the 1980s with the encouragement of the United States. The culture of Islamic militancy Lindh found spread through Pakistan and Afghanistan was fostered by militant ideologues turned holy warriors, such as Gulbuddin Hikmetyar and other mujaheddin supported by the United States against the Soviet Union in Afghanistan. Those and other dark ironies make Lindh's story not just intriguing, but telling in a deeper sense about the complexity of the conflicts the United States faces today, because the twisted coincidences of Lindh's story are not unique to the American experience in Afghanistan. Most of the hijackers of September 11 came from Saudi Arabia, a country outwardly allied with the United States. And this book goes to press just months after U.S. forces marched across Iraq in a campaign to strike down Saddam Hussein, a leader America once backed against Iran. Understanding Lindh, I hope, will help us, as Americans at war, to reflect on ourselves as well as the enemies we face.

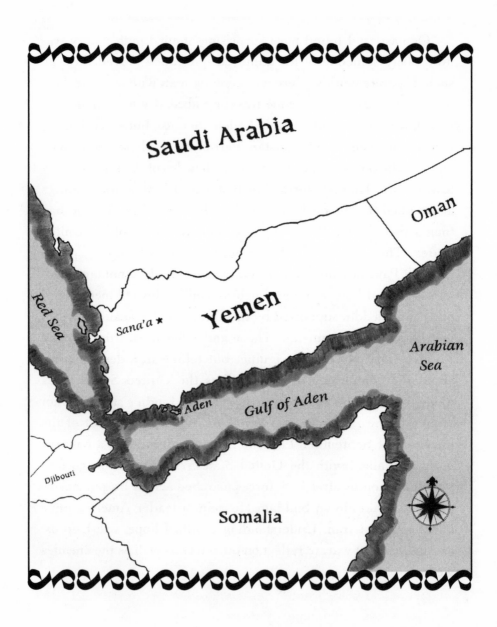

CHAPTER ONE

San Francisco to Sana'a

A STALE smell of sweat, spent cigarettes, and dust soaked with jet fuel washed over John Phillip Walker Lindh as he stepped wearily off a plane in Sana'a, Yemen, on July 1, 1998. A long string of connecting flights had taken him from his home near San Francisco to the Yemeni capital with five other study-abroad students on their way to the same Sana'a school. Jetlag weighed heavily on the group as they gathered up their luggage with the help of an official sent by the school to meet the bedraggled crew. Heading outside to waiting cars, the students walked through the dimly lit airport, which resembled a warehouse and rang like a grimy echo chamber with the voices of travelers speaking in languages from East Africa, the Middle East, and beyond.

From the air, Sana'a had looked like a petrified gingerbread city set in the central highlands of Yemen, where treeless mountains rise into desert skies. The architecture of Sana'a, dating back a millennium, is striking, unlike any other in the world. Tower houses made of basalt, brick, and mud stand up to eight stories high, dressed with ornate friezes and white gypsum plastering, which webs kaleidoscope windows of colored glass. One of the oldest cities in the world, Sana'a traces its origins back to the earliest of human settlements. Although increasingly modern, especially on the outskirts, much of Sana'a today has changed little in four centuries.

1

On the ground, however, the picturesque scenery served as a background to poverty and filth unlike anything the seventeen-year-old Lindh had seen growing up in the United States. The downtown traffic was a rolling twist of jalopies clattering and blaring their horns through crowds of pedestrians. Thin and dark, Yemeni men looked menacing, wearing the traditional broad, curved daggers called jambiyas in their belts, while the women glided like desert ghosts, veiled from head to foot in black. Lindh and the other students took in fleeting city scenes in the fading evening light as they drove from the airport to their new home at the Yemen Language Center campus, which sat in the center of town.

Behind high walls, on the outside, the school's twin walkup buildings matched the stately designs of the city's older architecture. Inside, the grounds were comfortably modern for the roughly fifty foreign students enrolled at the time, most of whom were young undergraduates taking accredited study-abroad courses ranging from short-term stays to a full year of immersion in the Arabic language. The center's auxiliary building had a recreation room with a dartboard and satellite television, as well as laundry facilities. In the main building, the dorms sat on floors above administrative offices and classrooms so small they could seat just five or six students at a time. On the sixth floor, above the student housing, a cluttered kitchen led to a rooftop mafraj, a sitting room lined with floor cushions overlooking the city. Lindh was given a corner room on the fifth floor of the main building. The space had little more than two mattresses on the floor, a couple of desks, and twin closets. On the night of his arrival, Lindh hardly talked to his roommate, another American, as he settled in and flopped onto a bed, drifting off to sleep with the first dull pangs of culture shock and homesickness sinking in.

Lindh's friends back at San Francisco's Mill Valley mosque

had tried to talk him out of going to Yemen, knowing he would likely have difficulty being so far away from home in such a strange place.

"We would have preferred he had gone somewhere else, Canada or maybe to England," said Abdullah Nana, one of Lindh's closest friends at the mosque.

Nana was one of the first people to befriend Lindh when he began showing up at the Mill Valley mosque in 1997. Lindh had only recently converted to Islam and adopted the name Suleyman al-Faris; Mill Valley was his first serious foray into the life of a practicing Muslim.

Sitting amid quiet, wooded hills, the mosque had been a Baptist church before the Muslim community in Mill Valley bought the simple clapboard building, tore out the pews, and remolded the main hall so that the new congregation would face east, toward Mecca. Five times a day Mill Valley Muslims gather for prayer, pulling into the blacktop parking lot in Acuras, sport utility vehicles, and shiny import sedans. Nana had, of course, noticed the teenage newcomer at the mosque, usually the only Caucasian present. Most of the worshipers had roots in India and elsewhere in South Asia, while a few others were African American.

Short and slender with a dark complexion, Nana spoke softly with a slight stammer. On his boyish face, he wore glasses with tiny frames and a heavy beard that gave him an elfin quality. If Santa Claus were based in Bombay, rather than the North Pole, his helpers might look something like Nana, who smiled cheerily when he talked about Lindh. "Just to make him feel welcome, I introduced myself and made friends with him," said Nana. Close in age, the two quickly bonded, spending many hours talking primarily about Islam before and after prayers at the mosque.

"The center place for our meeting and for our relationship

was basically the mosque," said Nana. "Most of our relationship was based on religion," he said. "We'd share our experiences, our goals, discussing the different aspects of Islam, the history of Islam, the different groups in Islam."

Nana, who lived with his family in the modest neighborhood around the mosque, would usually find Lindh praying there two or three times a week in 1997 and 1998, even though Lindh lived about nine miles away in San Anselmo with his mother, father, older brother, and younger sister. Lindh would take a bus, or ride his bike, for the long trip to the mosque. After praying and talking, Nana would usually give Lindh a ride home.

"Normally, every Friday I would see him," Nana said. "Sometimes we'd sit for a few hours after Friday, two or three hours we'd sit in the mosque, discuss different things."

Lindh had a lot on his mind regarding Islam. Lindh had been studying the religion, among others, on his own for some years before officially converting. As a Muslim his studies deepened, and he had involved conversations on many scholarly subjects with Nana that might have seemed strange from someone so young and so new to the faith.

"He definitely had a lot of interest," Nana said. "I remember he was very particular with his studies."

Lindh had been bookish from an early age. His parents, Frank Lindh and Marilyn Walker, named their second son John when he was born in February of 1981, two months after Beatle John Lennon died at the hands of a deranged fan. Both parents were big Lennon fans and named John partly in tribute to their favorite 1960s icon. Frank favored the name also because of a judge he looked up to, John Marshall.

When Lindh was born, his family, regular churchgoing Catholics, had settled into a comfortable rented house in a Maryland suburban neighborhood outside Washington, D.C., called Takoma Park. Marilyn stayed busy at home raising John, his older brother by three years, Connell, and later, their youngest child and only daughter, Naomi.

Frank, meanwhile, was working to launch a legal career and had enrolled at Georgetown Law, where he took evening classes after working day jobs to get through school. In those days, time and money were short for the family. Marilyn would shop in thrift stores, and the family car was one handed down from her parents. Occasionally, Marilyn worked retail jobs to bring in extra money. Despite the lean times, soon the family had enough to buy a house of its own in neighboring Silver Spring, Maryland, where the Lindhs joined a community of young professionals who mostly worked in law, academia, and lobbying. Some of Frank and Marilyn's neighbors seemed to hear echoes of the 1960s around the Lindh home, where the shelves were stocked with natural foods and medicines. But no one regarded the Lindhs as spacey hippie throwbacks, especially when Frank graduated cum laude from Georgetown Law.

Young John was performing comparatively well in school, albeit elementary school. He joined a special program at Kensington Parkwood Elementary, where children who displayed early academic talent sat in separate classes. The kids in the gifted program were self-described geeks and spent more time playing fantasy games among themselves than joining in playground sports like soccer. The cerebral play fit John, who was forced inside often because of asthma and allergies, which later caused him to miss school noticeably.

During all this, Frank was steadily moving up in the legal world. Shortly after his Georgetown graduation, he signed on with a series of local firms, as well as the Federal Energy Regulatory Commission. In 1989, as John turned eight, Frank got a job at a Washington law firm, LeBoeuf, Lamb, Leiby, and MacRae, which offered him a post in the firm's San Francisco office about two years later.

The family of five took up residence in San Anselmo, a more affordable corner of Marin County twenty miles north of San Francisco. Marin County has a deserved reputation as a haven for moneyed baby boomers with liberal leanings. On its shaded, rolling hills, blacktop roads curve through eucalyptus and redwood groves, carrying Porches, BMWs, and Range Rovers, as much as any other kind of car. Fleece vests appear as frequently as ponytails on men; Carlos Santana and Sean Penn occasionally appear on the streets.

The comforts meant little to John, however, as he struggled to adjust. He quickly lost touch with the tightly knit group he had known in the gifted program, and he changed schools repeatedly. John started fifth grade at one private school, then enrolled in a different one a year later, only to transfer again halfway through the year to a public school. An intestinal disorder added to the problems of his asthma and allergies, and he began to look sickly and miss still more class. In 1993, Frank and Marilyn took him out of school altogether, and he began to study at home with the help of a tutor.

There was trouble at home, though. Frank and Marilyn's marriage began showing strains that would later lead to their separation. The couple split in 1999, but Frank would later say he and Marilyn effectively separated six years earlier, about the time Lindh was spending most of his days in the house. The family problems and the years away from school didn't stunt Lindh's growth intellectually, however. In the fall of 1995, feeling healthy, Lindh began a freshman year at Redwood High School. He didn't stay long. After just one semester, Lindh left Redwood High and began studies at a special high school geared for gifted students like him.

Tamiscal High School, where Lindh enrolled, let students follow a ramped-up curriculum on their own time. There were no classes, only meetings between teachers and students, one on one, twice a week. Opened in 1991, Tamiscal High offered just the sort of progressive educational model one might expect in Marin County. Tamiscal was no place for teenage slackers, despite its loose approach to classroom time. A year's reading list alone was daunting enough to make most teens balk. But Lindh plunged into assigned texts about world cultures, poetry, politics, and religion.

In his free time, Lindh often turned to the Internet, surfing through Web sites as varied as his readings. He followed his interest in hip-hop music to rap sites, where he posted swaggering rhymes of his own. He flipped through Web pages devoted to conspiracy theories. And he browsed religious sites, including Islamic newsgroups where he logged on to type in questions about being Muslim. He wrote in asking if certain musical instruments were banned in Islam, whether it was okay to watch cartoons as a Muslim, and what sort of everyday things one was expected to forgo as a follower of the religion. Online, he searched out obscure books about Palestinians, Islam, and other subjects.

Among the books he read was the autobiography of Malcolm X, the African American civil rights activist whose religious epiphany in prison led to his conversion to Islam. Lindh, at age twelve, had seen Spike Lee's film version of the Malcolm X story, and his mother recalled his being struck by the images in one scene: Malcolm X's visit to Mecca during the annual Muslim pilgrimage known as the hajj, which draws followers from all over the globe. The vision of so many people from so many different places bowing before God together awed Lindh. Indeed, Malcolm X had some of his deepest spiritual moments while traveling in Arab lands to perform the hajj, a journey obligatory to all Muslims at least once in a lifetime.

"I only knew what I had left in America, and how it contrasted with what I found in the Muslim world," Malcolm X recalled in pages Lindh read. "About twenty of us Muslims who had finished the hajj were sitting in a huge tent on Mount Arafat. As a Muslim from America, I was the center of attention. They asked me what about the hajj had impressed me the most. One of several who spoke English asked; they translated my answers for the others. My answer to that question was not the one they expected, but it drove home my point. I said, 'The *brotherhood!* The people of all races, colors, from all over the world coming together as *one!* It proved to me the power of the One God.'"

By age sixteen, Lindh's interests in things like conspiracy theories and hip-hop had passed, and he became absorbed by Islam. That same year, he sold off his rap music collection, ended his studies at Tamiscal by taking a state high-school equivalency exam in lieu of earning a diploma, and delved further into his adopted religion. The curiosity that had driven his readings and Internet wanderings from age fourteen grew further still, and soon he began to seek out Muslims in his area. At the Islamic Center of Mill Valley, Lindh officially converted by presenting himself before two witnesses and voicing the shahada, the Islamic spiritual vow all Muslims take by declaring Allah the only god worthy of worship.

In his early days at the mosque, Lindh usually wore a shirt and pants. But soon he began dressing the part, donning flowing robes and pillbox hats of the kind worn by followers of Islam in South Asia, like Nana. Nana remembers seeing Lindh for the first time at the mosque in his new clothes, all white. Nana, who had also adopted the traditional dress about that time, was impressed.

"Four or five months after he accepted Islam, he started wearing the Islamic dress," Nana said. "You notice not everyone wears Islamic dress. It's a big step. It also shows his strength of character."

Lindh's outward expressions of faith, such as his dress and his practice of daily prayers, seemed to reflect his increasingly deeper religious exploration, which he fueled with a reading list he shaped himself. His readings plumbed many topics related to Islam, including biographies of the prophet Mohammed, accounts of his early companions, and treatises on Islamic law. He was quickly becoming a self-styled, nascent religious scholar and told Nana that he was considering pursuing Islamic theology. Nana had ideas about becoming an Islamic scholar too, and their common interest led to many theological discussions. In their talks at the mosque, Nana and Lindh would discuss such things as the sunnah, the doings and sayings of the prophet, whose life is seen as a guiding example for all Muslims. The sunnah are spelled out in writings called the hadith, the recorded sunnah — what Mohammed's followers observed of the things he did and said during his lifetime. Nana and Lindh would discuss the hadith too, taking up a long-running debate in Islam over the authenticity of certain written records of the prophet.

They also discussed different schools of thought and theological trends. Lindh, it seemed to Nana, leaned toward a revivalist interpretation of Islam that stemmed largely from a reformist movement called classic Salafiyah, which emerged in the Arab world around the ninth century. Salafiyah adherents of the era thought that Muslims had gone adrift, taking up practices that contravened the original teachings of Islam, such as the worship of saints and prayer at burial grounds. Early Salafiyah thinkers, such as Ibn Taymiyah, called on Muslims to reject any religious practices without roots in the Koran, the hadith, and the sunnah. Theirs was a protestant movement, somewhat like Christianity's Lutheranism, taken up most successfully by a cleric named Muhammad Ibn 'Abd al-Wahhab. In the 1700s, al-Wahhab galvanized the theological thinking into a politico-religious doctrine known today as Wahhabism, a form of Islam still widely practiced on the Arabian Peninsula, where it was founded. Nana's interpretation of Islam was slightly more relaxed, in tune with his South Asian roots, whereas Lindh's approach to Islam had a more Arab flavor to it. In Nana's opinion, Lindh, the new convert, took his adopted faith more seriously than many in the Mill Valley community with generational Muslim roots. Nana was always eager to introduce Lindh to other Muslims he knew, because he viewed Lindh as a model example for religious devotion.

"By watching him, maybe they would come more to the Islamic way," Nana said.

Nana and Lindh had their own clique of five or so other teens from the mosque who would sometimes hang out together, like other teenagers.

"Once we went to go play miniature golf," Nana said, describing with a laugh how a group of six from the mosque hit a put-put course, teaming up three on three. "All of us actually, we weren't really golfers."

They weren't really basketball players either. At least Lindh wasn't the day some of the Mill Valley brothers picked up a game of hoops.

"Me and him were both wearing Islamic dress at that time," Nana said. Nana took off his long shirt to play, but Lindh stayed dressed and watched from the sidelines.

Lindh seemed at home with other Muslims, but he was finding it difficult to be with others away from the mosque. Lindh told Nana that on at least one occasion strangers had jeered at him for his Islamic clothes at the bus stop. On Christmas Eve in 1997, his first holiday season as a Muslim, Lindh turned up at the mosque, saying he had to get out of the house, where, of course, his family was celebrating a holiday he no longer observed. He wound up spending the night with Nana and others, sleeping in the mosque, as some Muslims do during the Islamic holy month of Ramadan, which that year overlapped with Christmas.

As his exploration into Islam deepened, Lindh began to contemplate traveling to Muslim lands to further his study of the religion. One of the reasons Lindh wanted to go to Yemen, he later told Nana, was that he wanted to be in a Muslim country where he could more easily practice Islam. Although Lindh was serious about learning Arabic, specifically Yemeni Arabic, Nana remembered that Lindh's desire to be in a Muslim country was the "main reason" for his going overseas.

"He didn't want to stay in this environment any longer," Nana said.

To Nana, Lindh's desire to live in an Islamic country was yet one more show of unusually strong faith, like the clothes, the prayers, and the burgeoning beard he wore.

"Within a year of accepting Islam, he had already left the country for the sake of Islam," Nana said. "I mean, he's going from a first-world country to a third-world country."

Lindh had decided to go to Yemen because he hoped to learn the country's literary style of spoken Arabic, widely regarded as the form of Arabic that most closely resembles the original language of the Koran. Lindh had checked out language schools in Yemen online and decided on the Yemen Language Center, where he signed up for a year-long Arabic program.

Frank and Marilyn had offered no objection to their younger son's decisions to leave Tamiscal and adopt Islam. Instead, they were supportive of the religious exploration. Marilyn would sometimes drive Lindh to Friday prayers, and both parents tried to show patience when he said he was changing his name to Suleyman al-Faris. The idea of watching their youngest son go off to Yemen alone at age seventeen was more difficult to swallow, but they remained supportive and agreed to bankroll his studies abroad.

His friends at the Mill Valley mosque put on brave faces too, despite some of their worries. Lindh, they feared, would find life hard in Yemen, since he had never visited any third-world countries. Plus, Lindh didn't have a clue about Arabic, much less Yemeni Arabic. And Yemen did not seem like the sort of place where one would find many English speakers who could help him overcome the language barrier.

"It was his decision. Basically, we supported him in his decision," Nana said.

Nana and about ten other Muslim young men from the Mill Valley mosque even threw Lindh a small going-away party shortly before he left. Over a quiet lunch at a house near the Mill Valley mosque, Nana and the other brothers made a special effort to encourage Lindh on his journey. They rallied behind him in the hope of giving him some spiritual strength for the long trip. They told him that if one dies seeking Islamic knowledge, he dies a martyr, just as one does in war.

"I remember we were telling him about the different virtues right before he left, just to encourage him," Nana said. "It's a great reward, actually."

Lindh didn't seem to have the nervous feelings shared by his family and friends as he said his good-byes to the Mill Valley brothers. Nana remembers Lindh being excited.

"I think he was looking for it as a new opportunity, as a new chance to go to a Muslim country," Nana said.

☪

On his first full day in Yemen, Lindh awoke to early light aglow in reds, oranges, greens, and blues from his room's high, colored windows. Outside, the welling echoes of the early call to prayer, or azzan, sounded from countless Sana'a mosques, overlapping Arabic chants bellowing from loudspeakers atop minarets. The azzan filled the city all at once, as it does every day, marking dawn with a beautiful solemnity. The sound must have been welcome music to Lindh, who dressed in his robes and sandals for a school outing.

Downstairs, Lindh and a group of other newcomers joined a school official, who was to show them a place to change money in nearby Tahrir Square, where the first of several embarrassments for which Lindh would later be remembered at the school unfolded. For starters, Lindh's Islamic garb seemed strange to his fellow students, mostly Westerners who dressed in fashionable American or European styles. And Lindh's insistence on being called Suleyman drew snickers from the students, as did his beard, which by then had grown in fairly well for a teenager.

The school group, numbering about half a dozen, filed out of the center's gates and down a shady strip of road toward the square, a crowded sweep of paved open space ringed by storefronts. Lindh and the others exchanged their dollars and pounds for Yemeni riyals, as a crowd of beggars gathered around them. Pocketing wads of local currency, the students edged back to the entrance of the square through a growing throng, with a few of the foreigners giving out small alms to the locals. Quickly, most of the students stopped offering handouts to avoid a scene as the crowd of beggars swelled. Not Lindh, though. He held up a fist full of the Yemeni riyals, colored brightly in pinks and greens, peeling off large notes that amounted to half a day's wages to Yemen's poor, who are accustomed to getting a pittance, if anything, from rare visitors to one of the world's poorest countries.

Onlookers watched and drew closer as Lindh gave out more money. Suddenly, the idle crowd grew into a mob pressing toward Lindh, and he found himself standing at the head of a jostling line of people reaching for his money. The other students stepped away annoyed, leaving Lindh groping through the gathering confusion he had created, struggling to keep up with the group. At the bottom of the square, the other visiting students followed their school guide on a left turn that led back to the language center. Lindh, swept up in the crush, turned right and lost his classmates as he ambled east, toward the maze of houses in the Old City, where he drifted for eight hours, lost and alone after the beggars finally fell away.

The honking cacophony of outer Sana'a gives way to a hushed calm in the Old City, where narrow alleyways deep in shade carry the sounds of playing children and the murmurs of passersby. The few cars and motorcycles in the Old City seem out of place amid the etched stones and carved wooden doors around markets redolent of dates, raisins, and spices piled heavily into burlap sacks. The calls to prayer coming from the soaring minarets ring more loudly in the Old City's quiet as well, drawing shuffling masses to overflowing mosques. Lindh stopped to pray at several mosques before eventually wandering back late that night to the center, where word of the spectacle he staged in the square earlier had created something of a buzz. The students, whom Lindh initially puzzled and amused with his memorable first impressions, soon grew to see him as something of an annoying joke. The following weeks did little to help his reputation.

The days at the language center's coed campus started at eight in the morning, when the teachers, mostly locals, began lessons in the small classrooms. The first round of Arabic classes lasted two hours, and then the students were given a short break. Lessons resumed at the ring of a school bell around ten in the morning and went until about noon, when the language center's school day officially ended, leaving students free for the afternoon and evening.

After classes, most of the students relaxed on campus or explored the city between study sessions. Unlike Lindh, few were concerned with the calls to prayer sounding five times a day. Lindh would urge the other Muslims at the center to join him for prayers, but he found few takers and went out on his own.

Lindh prayed at mosques near the center, but was surprised to see some Yemenis skipping calls on occasion. Lindh had assumed that in a Muslim country everyone would be going to every prayer. Some Yemenis, like Muslims in Islamic countries everywhere, sometimes miss a prayer or two and go about the day's business, or simply chew qat, a leafy plant with mildly narcotic effects. In conversations with other students at the center, Lindh expressed disdain over the widespread Yemeni practice of chewing. And he was taken aback by what he saw as a lack of piety among Yemenis who skipped prayers to chew. The students laughed Lindh off whenever he talked about the importance of religious observance. They saw in Lindh a walking caricature of a Muslim, someone who strutted every Islamic stereotype. Lindh held them in a similar low regard. Lindh felt the other students offended local sensibilities by acting as they normally would in America or Europe while they were in an Islamic country. He even went so far one day as to hang a note on the door of a dorm room on his floor, addressed "Dear Inhabitants of This Room," asking the foreign students inside to "Please abstain from getting naked in front of the window. Our neighbors from the apartment building across the street have complained to Sabri, who has ignored them. However, this is not a matter to be taken lightly. Some of our neighbors have threatened to shoot Sabri and/or the inhabitants of this room and the room next to it. Please pass this message on to the inhabitants of room #2, and thank you for your decency." Sabri Saleem, the school's owner and headmaster referred to in the note, had never been threatened by his neighbors and had no doubt that Lindh had written the unsigned missive.

Within a week of arriving, Lindh, the only student who

seemed discontent with the center, had complained to Saleem. The first time the two met, the young American had visited Saleem's ground-floor corner office one afternoon to express his unhappiness with the center's program. Saleem took the complaints to mean that Lindh somehow wanted or expected the school to have an Islamic element to the curriculum and that Lindh felt uneasy with the coed atmosphere.

"I told him, look, this is a language school for both females and males," Saleem remembered, speaking in early November of 2002, some four years after Lindh's arrival.

"This is not an Islamic school," said Saleem, a native Yemeni with graying curly hair who wears tailored suits more often than local garb. Thin and smooth-skinned with a slight mustache, Saleem, a former Peace Corps worker, strives to make his school comfortable for paying Western students of Arabic. The center has no religious courses, which those enrolled generally aren't seeking anyway.

"We teach Arabic as a foreign language," Saleem told Lindh. "We teach Arabic language and culture, that's our program. So we are not specialized in Islamic studies."

The two must have somehow misunderstood each other, because Lindh remembered the conversation differently. Lindh was just trying to say that he felt like the Arabic lessons offered at the school did not live up to the program as billed on the Web site. He had no qualms about women being at the center and had never expected any sort of religious instruction. The conversation ended sourly, recalled Saleem, who began to wonder about this latest American pupil.

Lindh was not the first Islamic convert to enroll at the center. In the fifteen years Saleem had been in business, perhaps a dozen or so newfound Muslims from the United States and Europe had appeared at his school. Many of them held conservative views on Islam, a common trait among converts, but all had seemed at ease with the school's secular program and relaxed atmosphere, socializing with the other students without trouble. Lindh was different.

"I've seen other American Muslim students," Saleem said. "Suleyman was a completely different picture. I think he did not like the environment. He was isolated. He did not mix with other students."

The only time Saleem and the other faculty members saw Lindh was when he was in class or on his way out the door, heading to an area mosque for prayers.

Saleem had heard about the scene in Tahrir Square. He had also heard that the other students were having trouble with Lindh, but that they didn't voice complaints to Saleem in hopes of keeping Lindh out of trouble. Saleem heard one rumor that Lindh would try to wake Muslim students for the early and late calls to prayer, chastising anyone unwilling to go to the mosque when the azzans sounded well after midnight and shortly before dawn.

"He was trying to interfere with the other students, telling them what to do," Saleem said. "He did not get along with anyone."

The center's students took Lindh in stride. When Lindh did talk to classmates, he spoke of traveling to Yemen's north, where he hoped to study with Islamic clerics teaching the conservative brand of Islam he saw as the truer path. As a result of his religious fervor, behind Lindh's back, his classmates jokingly referred to him as Yusuf Islam, the Islamic name adopted by Cat Stevens, the singer who had turned Muslim. Lindh had indeed withdrawn, and his isolation intensified. He spent long hours at his desk studying the Koran and his Arabic lessons, while the other students mingled. Inwardly, he was feeling depressed, alienated, and disenchanted.

The concerns Nana and others had about his traveling to a third-world country turned out to be well founded. The poverty in the streets of Sana'a disturbed him, and the new sights, sounds, and smells, so unlike those of Marin County, left him feeling despondent and melancholy. The situation at the Yemen Language Center upset Lindh the most, however. Lindh had wanted an intensive Arabic immersion program. Instead, he found himself at a school where students spoke more English than Arabic, and the classroom pace moved as slowly as foreign language study at college campuses in the West. Lindh felt cheated and wanted to leave, so he began exploring other schools in Sana'a. Unbeknownst to Saleem at the time, Lindh began spending many nights a week away from the center at the city's largest Islamic university, Jami'at al-Iman. Lindh went missing from the center several nights a week during his first few weeks in Yemen. He kept his things in his room and showed up for class regularly, but would disappear in the evenings, taking advantage of Saleem's adult approach to dorm life at the center.

"Students are free," said Saleem, who enforces no curfew and lets students come and go without checks. "They can do whatever they want. This is not a prison."

For most students, the center's modern amenities were a refuge from other possible places to stay in Sana'a, and Saleem recalled having no trouble with the policy until Lindh came.

After roughly a month of living at the center, Lindh told Sabri he wanted to move into the student housing at al-Iman, but continue taking Arabic classes at Saleem's school. Saleem initially was open to the idea.

"I said I have no problem, but you'd better communicate with your family," Saleem said, recalling how he told Lindh to put something in writing to formalize his request.

On August 8, Lindh gave Saleem a handwritten note saying he "would like to leave the Yemen Language Center housing but continue my studies in the school. Because I intend to take classes in my new residence, the Jami'at al-Iman, I would appreciate your flexibility in changing class times." He signed the note, "John Lindh (Suleyman)."

While considering Lindh's request to move out, Saleem thought back to when the boy's mother had called him to talk about the school before he enrolled, saying she wanted her son to take classes only at his center. Lindh, his mother told Saleem, had expressed interest in studying in Yemen, prompting his parents to research schools. Sabri's came highly recommended, and Lindh's parents agreed to let their son study in Sana'a on the condition that he enroll at Sabri's center and nowhere else. They registered him for a year's courses and paid half of the $6,000 tuition fees up front. Lindh seemed okay with the arrangements at the time, despite the discontent he showed after arriving. In the end, Saleem decided against letting Lindh go, because he felt doing so would break the agreement Lindh had made with his parents, an agreement Saleem had become the keeper of.

"He came under my name," Saleem said. "He was in my house, in the center, in my facilities. I was responsible for him."

When Saleem told Lindh he couldn't change housing, Lindh grew angry. He told Saleem he wanted to quit the school altogether, and the two began arguing about tuition money. After some back and forth, Lindh dropped the matter and told Saleem that he would serve out the remaining ten-week term. After Lindh left the office, Saleem didn't hear any more complaints. Shortly after that tense conversation, about six weeks into his courses, Lindh emptied his room and disappeared.

"He just ran away," said Saleem, who went looking for Lindh

immediately. Saleem knew Lindh had likely remained in the city, since government roadblocks on the outskirts rarely allowed anyone to pass through without an official travel permit. He also doubted Lindh had fallen victim to one of Yemen's notorious kidnappings, which usually happen in the northern tribal areas. For four days, Saleem combed the Sana'a mosques and bazaars, checked another nearby school, the Center for Arabic Language and Eastern Studies, and, finally, visited al-Iman, where he found his runaway American pupil living with a host of other foreign students enrolled there. With a friend, Saleem had made the twenty-minute drive to the campus, a nondescript cinderblock complex with separate dorms for men and women, classroom buildings, a cafeteria, and a mosque. On the grounds, Saleem asked students he saw if they knew a young American named Suleyman. They did. Lindh, Saleem was told, was living on campus in a dorm with another foreign student from Africa. Saleem went to the room, but Lindh was away. So Saleem waited on campus until the evening call to prayer sounded, betting that Lindh would come to the mosque.

"The only time you can catch him is in the mosque," Saleem said.

Lindh showed. After prayers, Saleem pulled him aside.

"You really need to call your parents," said Saleem, who also urged Lindh to come by the center to discuss things.

Lindh told Saleem he would call home, but made no promise to come back to his center for any reason before quickly turning away.

"He didn't like me," Saleem said.

Saleem then called Lindh's mother himself and followed up with a faxed letter dated September 5, 1998. Saleem told Lindh's mother how he had found her son at al-Iman:

I was also informed that there is no phone number at the university that he could be contacted by. When I spoke with him I told him that he must do two things: return to the YLC to discuss his study situation and phone his parents. To date, he has not come to talk to me and I am unsure if he has contacted you. Previously, John informed me that he was interested in moving out of the YLC dorm and leaving the program of Arabic study here to study at an institution where he felt more comfortable and where there would be a strong Islamic emphasis. I told him that this decision was fine, but that we would have to review his YLC study agreement to check on the terms for early withdrawal. This was all prior to my knowledge that you did not want him to study anywhere besides the YLC.

Saleem went on to say that he had contacted the U.S. Embassy about Lindh.

Unfortunately there is no way for them to get involved, however there are several other options in this situation. First, it would greatly help if you wrote a letter to me explaining that John is to study exclusively at the YLC as we discussed. I can show this letter to him and see if he acknowledges its content. If he refuses it then I can ask him to leave the country and return home on your behalf. If he refuses to leave then I can ask the government to get involved, in which case they could revoke his visa and personally ask him to leave. One other scenario could occur that you should also consider. If he agrees to study at the YLC, he may also decide to study simultaneously at the Islamic school. I am not sure how you feel about this, but it sounded like this was what John intended to do when he initially decided to leave the YLC housing. Please keep these options in mind or offer your own, and we will do our best to get this resolved. If you have any questions or new information please do not hesitate to contact me.

Lindh's mother did contact Saleem—and said she had decided to let her son drop out of the Yemen Language Center and continue his studies at al-Iman. Lindh sounded happy at the school, she told Saleem.

"I just left it there," Saleem said.

CHAPTER TWO

A New Kind of School

THROUGHOUT the 1980s and 1990s, Osama bin Laden looked to Yemen, his ancestral homeland, for young recruits willing to take up military campaigns for the sake of Islam. An estimated three thousand Yemenis traveled to Afghanistan during the 1980s, as bin Laden and others, including the United States, endeavored to aid the Afghan mujaheddin, or holy warriors, in their insurgency against Soviet occupation. Like scores of other foreign fighters, often called jihadis, the Yemenis who got involved in the Afghan conflict eventually returned to their native country. The flock of veteran holy warriors in Yemen became known as the Arab Afghans, a community that formed part of the political base for conservative Islamist figures like Abdel Meguid al-Zindani, a leader in Yemen's second largest political party, Islah, and longtime head of al-Iman University, Lindh's new home.

Jami'at al-Iman, translated as the University of Faith, sits amid dusty hills scattered with unfinished construction sites in a web of dirt roads on the outskirts of Sana'a. As of November 2002, guards armed with Kalashnikovs blocked the entrance to al-Iman, where school officials refused to grant a campus visit or cooperate with outside interviews of students and faculty who knew Lindh.

Numbering some 4,000, students at al-Iman hail from more

than fifty countries. With funding from the Yemeni government, as well as donors from the Persian Gulf and Turkey, al-Zindani shaped the school as a conservative answer to the university system in Cairo, where strident Islamist thinkers consider the education too westernized to be considered properly Islamic. As a measure of comparison, Cairo could be seen as the seat of the Arab world's Ivy League schools, with institutions such as Ain Shams, Al-Azhar, and Cairo University. Sana'a, on the other hand, hosts something like the Islamic version of Bob Jones University with al-Zindani's al-Iman.

Al-Zindani's own teachings serve as the touchstone for al-Iman's overriding religious curriculum and the political tenor of campus life. In sermons, al-Zindani has suggested that President George W. Bush plotted with Jews to stage the September 11 attacks and used them as a war cry against Muslims around the world. In other rants, al-Zindani has called on Yemeni authorities to end counterterrorism cooperation with the United States, labeled backers of the U.S. campaign in Afghanistan as infidels, and insisted that bin Laden, a man he has called a friend since the 1970s, is not a terrorist.

When Lindh first began staying on the al-Iman campus, he could not fully take in al-Zindani's dogma, since he could still speak no Arabic. However, the jihadi ranks drawn to al-Iman replaced the Western classmates Lindh had known briefly at the Yemen Language Center. Among the students at al-Iman, Lindh met several young men who had fought in places like Chechnya and Afghanistan, and they told him of their experiences of jihad. In this radical environment, Lindh was turned on to English translations of jihadi literature, chiefly the writings of slain holy warrior and scholar Shaykh Abdullah Azzam.

Ever an independent student, Lindh had never found a spiritual mentor for his Islamic studies, not in Mill Valley and certainly not at the Yemen Language Center. He might have at al-Iman, as scores of other young men did in al-Zindani. But the language barrier kept Lindh from absorbing virtually anything beyond the level of beginner's Arabic. In Shaykh Abdullah Azzam, however, Lindh discovered a leader and a guide, a religious intellectual who thought deeply and felt strongly about how to interpret the modern world according to Islamic principles and backed up his theological arguments with an academic's reasoning. Degreed with a Ph.D. from al-Azhar University in Cairo, Azzam eschewed Islamic scholarly matters. He focused instead on the state of Muslims at war, an issue he knew firsthand from fighting against the Soviets in Afghanistan.

Azzam's two foremost writings, *Join the Caravan* and *Defense of the Muslim Lands*, posit jihadi manifestos and read at once like religious inspiration and a sort of instruction manual. Some 1980s editions of *Join the Caravan* even listed phone numbers for the recruitment office at Azzam's Peshawar, Pakistan, base of operations. Readers willing to make the journey could sign on with Makhtab al-Khidimat, a mujaheddin organization Azzam founded with the help of bin Laden and others. Both *Join the Caravan* and *Defense of the Muslim Lands* have been widely translated and printed in small booklets, which can be found in Islamic bookstores even in San Francisco.

In his writings, Azzam speaks of the ummah, a concept of Islamic union that transcends national boundaries and binds all Muslims together as one nation. In *Defense of the Muslim Lands*, Azzam argues that muslims who fail to protech the ummah fail their god:

[The] sin upon this present generation, for not advancing towards Afghanistan, Palestine, the Philippines, Kashmir, Lebanon, Chad, Eritria, etc, is greater than the sin inherited from the loss of the lands which have previously fallen into the possession of the disbelievers. . . . Moreover, our occupying enemies are very deceptive and execute programs to extend their power in these regions. If we were to resolve these dilemmas we would resolve a great deal of complications. Their protection is the protection for the whole ummah.

Refusing to defend the ummah with force, Azzam contended, equalled a sinful transgression comparable to forgoing daily prayers or fasting during the holy month of Ramadan. If Muslims face a threat, Azzam's doctrine goes, then the Muslims of that area are obligated to fight a defensive jihad. If the locals cannot muster enough force to defend themselves, then Muslims in neighboring lands must come to their aid. If the threat still cannot be beaten back, the responsibility falls to Muslims in the next nearest lands, and so on, until eventually Muslims everywhere are called up in defense of the ummah.

"Whoever can, from among the Arabs, fight jihad in Palestine, then he must start there," Azzam writes. "If he is not capable, then he must set out for Afghanistan. For the rest of the Muslims, I believe they should start their jihad in Afghanistan."

Though Azzam was assassinated in 1989 in Peshawar, he lived on in the jihadi world with mythic status. Throughout the 1990s, a new generation of young Muslims looked to his writings for inspiration and to his peers, such as bin Laden, for leadership with regard to what they saw as crises in such places as Kashmir, Chechnya, and Afghanistan, where the Taliban's insistence that it was forming a pure Muslim state was in tune with another point Azzam stresses in *Join the Caravan*. In that book, Azzam calls the establishment and preservation of Islamic states a vital Muslim need.

This homeland will not come about without an organized Islamic movement which perseveres consciously and realistically upon

Jihad, and which regards fighting as a decisive factor and as a protective cover. The Islamic movement will not be able to establish the Islamic community except through a common, people's Jihad which has the Islamic movement as its beating heart and deliberating mind.

The state of Afghanistan was a distant thought for Lindh during his first trip to Yemen. However, Azzam's message of the obligatory duty of jihad for Muslims was becoming important to him as an element of his religious identity nonetheless. In further pages of *Join the Caravan*, Lindh read about Azzam's belief that anyone "who looks into the state of the Muslims today will find that their greatest misfortune is their abandonment of Jihad. . . . Because of that, the tyrants have gained dominance over the Muslims in every aspect and in every land." Azzam scoffs at Muslims who put work and study ahead of jihad:

Weighty matters and grave, painful disasters have befallen the Muslims. So stop talking about food and styles of speech, and instead, tell me about this important matter and what the Muslims have prepared for it. Matters which, were they to be contemplated by a child, the child's appearance would become that of one aged. . . .

What then do you think about the millions of Muslims who are being humiliated with dreadful persecution, and are living the lives of cattle? They cannot repel attacks on their honor, lives and properties. Nay, such a man cannot even have his own way in growing his beard because it is an obvious sign of Islam.

Nor, in fact, is he free to have his wife wear the long garments required by Islam because it is a crime for which he may be seized anywhere and at any time. Nor can he teach the Koran to three Muslim youths in the mosque because it is an illegal gathering according to the law of the ignorant. Nay, in some of the countries which are called Islamic, he cannot even have his wife cover her hair, nor can he prevent the intelligence officers from taking his daughter by the hand in the depths of night, under the cover of pitch-darkness, to wherever they wish. Can he refuse a command issued by the evil authorities in which he provides a cheap sacrifice on the altar of the whims of this tyrant?

Are these millions not living lives of despicable subjugation, and do the angels not take their souls while they are wronging themselves? What then will be their reply when the angels ask them: "What was the matter with you?" Will they not say, "We were weak and oppressed in the land?" Weakness is not an excuse before the Lord of the Worlds. In fact, it is a crime making the one committing it deserving of Hell. But Allah has excused those of advanced years, the small children and the women who neither find any scheme for liberation, nor know the path to the Land of Honor, nor are able to emigrate to the land of Islam or to arrive at the base for Jihad.

I shall turn my face away from a land which has made my tongue ineffective and locked up my heart. A man's clear resolution and common sense dictate that he turn away from the sun's glare. Jihad and emigration to Jihad have a deep-rooted role which cannot be separated from the constitution of this religion. A religion which does not have Jihad cannot become established in any land, nor can it strengthen its frame. The steadfast Jihad, which is one of the innermost constituents of this religion and which has its weight in the Scales of the Lord of the Worlds, is not a contingent phenomenon peculiar to the period in which the Koran was revealed; it is in fact a necessity accompanying the caravan which this religion guides.

Azzam's message, essentially, was that no able follower of Islam was exempt from jihad, especially given the situation faced by Muslims struggling in conflicts scattered across the globe in his time. Azzam argues in his writings that to fight on behalf of Islam is not just noble and worthy, but absolutely necessary in order to fulfill one's religious obligations. Azzam's thoughts on jihad, to Lindh, opened a previously unknown realm of religious duty. It was as though Lindh suddenly learned that being a Muslim required not just one holy pilgrimage in a lifetime, but two. Lindh was beginning to feel that to be a true follower of Islam, one eventually had to take up jihad in some form, just as sure as all able Muslims were required to make the journey to Mecca and follow other basic Islamic observances.

While Lindh took Azzam's writings to heart, the idea that he could become a warrior seemed farfetched. He recognized that with his gangly build, bookish nature, and frequent bouts of illness, he hardly had the makings of a soldier of God. And in Yemen, there was no pressing conflict that might demand his service. So Lindh busied himself at al-Iman with Arabic classes and his own readings. He struggled with the immersion, but he preferred this school with its difficulties to the others he had tried. During this time, Lindh also began thinking more about where and how he would continue his Islamic studies and coming up with vague ideas about eventually becoming a doctor or perhaps a professional translator of Arabic texts. He thought about studying, when his Arabic had improved enough, at a university in Medina; he felt he shouldn't enter a holy city like Medina until he had some mastery of Arabic and a deeper understanding of the Koran, however. The long-term goals and the everyday routine with friends at al-Iman contented Lindh, and he wrote many upbeat notes home, keeping in close touch with his family. Some of his e-mails home reflected al-Iman's political culture, which was colored by the widespread suspicion and anger felt by many in the Muslim world toward the United States—feelings Lindh began to share.

On September 23, 1998, Lindh wrote a telling note home in which he doubted the involvement of Islamic militants in recent bombing attacks against U.S. embassies in East Africa. On August 7 of that year, car bombs exploded almost simultaneously outside the U.S. embassies in Nairobi, Kenya, and Dar es Salaam, Tanzania. The twin blasts killed at least 220 people, most of them poor Africans. The United States immediately blamed the strike on bin Laden, and, in 2001, a federal court in New York convicted four accused al-Qaida operatives of staging the attacks. But to Lindh, at the time, the bombings seemed "far more likely to have been carried out by the American government than by any Muslims."

In a later e-mail, Lindh wrote his mother, half jokingly, that she should move to England: "I really don't understand what your big attachment to America is all about. What has America ever done for anybody?" In yet another e-mail, he expressed his view that the United States had sparked the Gulf War. Lindh believed that an American official had "heavily encouraged" Saddam Hussein to invade Kuwait. As time passed, it appeared that Lindh's environment and the ideas to which he was being exposed at al-Iman began to impact his view of global politics.

While happy in his initial months at al-Iman, Lindh still experienced troubles. He had stayed in Yemen illegally after the school had failed to get a new Yemeni visa for him, despite his enrollment. And his parents, particularly his mother, continued to press Lindh to come home for a visit. By the spring of 1999, he had decided to leave Yemen. Lindh went to catch a flight out, but was stopped at the Sana'a airport when immigration officials spotted his expired visa, something Yemeni authorities take very seriously. Yemeni officials told Lindh he could not leave the country unless the person who originally got him a visa vouched for him. This forced Lindh to return once more to the Yemen Language Center to face Saleem.

On the evening of April 26, 1999, Lindh returned to Saleem's office, this time with an immigration official. Saleem had assumed that the visa he initially got for Lindh would be renewed by al-Iman after Lindh took up classes there. But officials at al-Iman had failed to complete Lindh's paperwork, Lindh told Saleem. Saleem could have been angry or frustrated with Lindh, this American who had caused him so much headache. Instead, he felt pity. Lindh looked wan and unwashed in his robes as he pleaded with Saleem to write a formal letter freeing him from the center's charge, thereby allowing him to leave the country. Saleem obliged gladly, especially seeing Lindh sick and desperate, longing to go home. With a note and a wave, Saleem freed Lindh, who spent one night more in Sana'a in government custody before catching a departing flight.

☪

Nana saw Lindh again at the Mill Valley mosque shortly after his return. Nana was also on break from studying abroad in South Africa, and the two sat for an hour, swapping stories about their travels. Lindh was unhappy about being back. All the things that had made Lindh want to leave America in the first place were, of course, waiting for him when he returned, largely against his wishes, at the insistence of his family. While he had found Yemen difficult at times, he nonetheless preferred the Islamic culture there to American society, and the contrast of the two worlds must have seemed especially sharp upon his return to California. Mill Valley's stress-management clinics, day spas, and designer stores look like sick vanities compared to the scarcity and want in Yemen. The wooded hills Lindh had once called home can seem like an eternal summer camp for the wealthy to an outsider, a perspective Lindh would have understood after growing comfortable among foreigners at al-Iman. Outside the tiny Islamic communities he found in Bay Area mosques, Lindh saw little, if anything, around him in California that would have eased him spiritually. More importantly, Lindh felt he was losing ground in his Arabic studies.

Lindh told Nana he was eager to return to Yemen, but his parents wanted him to stay home, as the family was going through some difficult changes. Frank and Marilyn's marriage had grown more strained while Lindh was in Yemen, where he first found out his parents were separating by e-mail. In the winter, while Lindh was away, his father had moved out of the house after telling the family he was gay. Lindh mentioned none of this to Nana or others at the Mill Valley mosque. Lindh seemed concerned most of all, Nana recalled, about his Arabic, which he felt was leaving him with every day he spent in the United States. Lindh also told Nana that he was finding studying at al-Iman difficult, since there was virtually no English spoken on campus. He was beginning to wonder if perhaps he should find a school where teachers could speak with him in English.

"When he came back, I remember him discussing his experiences," Nana said. "At that time he mentioned that he was looking for an English medium."

Nana suggested Pakistan, where English is the official language and Arabic is widely taught in the many Islamic schools. Nana and Lindh didn't get a chance to share much time together, really. Nana headed back to South Africa about two weeks after he saw Lindh that day in the mosque, and Lindh was spending less time there. Instead, he was taking a longer bus ride regularly into San Francisco, where he began spending days at the San Francisco Islamic Center on Jones Street and at another mosque nearby on Sutter.

Both mosques sit downtown in an area known as the Tenderloin, where topless bars, sex shops, and seedy hotels foot the glassy skyscraper canyons of the financial district. The San Francisco Islamic Center that Lindh favored is on the third floor of an old building on the corner of Market and Jones, overlooking a donut shop and an adult movie theater. With a corner view, the mosque's huge plate windows occasionally catch the glint of a spark from passing trolleys, which ring and bang on the street below alongside buses and cars. The walls are bare, except for one picture of Jerusalem. For most of the day, the place is quiet and bright, with light floating down from milky skylights as pigeons reel in flocks over the roof. Then, a softly voiced call to prayer sounds, loud enough only for those inside to hear, and followers trickle in and take off their shoes.

On a Friday, the Jones Street mosque has a following much larger and more diverse than the Mill Valley mosque. Many Yemenis live in the area, particularly around the Sutter Street mosque, a much smaller, windowless building just a few blocks away. While Lindh wound up spending increasingly more time in San Francisco, he continued to visit the Mill Valley mosque regularly. Nana was gone, but his other friends were there, and he met still more during those months.

Khizar Hayat was in a hurry when he first met Lindh at the Mill Valley mosque in early September 1999. At the time, Hayat, a Pakistani, was in the Bay Area as one of his last stops during nine months of missionary work in connection with Tablighi Jamaat, an Islamic evangelical group avowedly peaceable and apolitical.

"Actually there was no time for us when I met him," said Hayat, who recalled, as he sat in his hometown of Bannu, Pakistan, roughly four months after the American's capture with the Taliban, how he had come to know Lindh.

Hayat wore his straight, wiry beard stiff and long beneath his sharp nose and wide brown eyes. Under his white prayer cap, Hayat's impassive manner was etched deeply in the lines of his broad, weathered forehead, which made him look much older than his thirty-two years.

Talking after midday prayers in a Bannu madrassa, Hayat appeared aloof and dismissive of virtually everyone around him. He muttered when he talked and easily grew impatient with questions. He had initially refused to be interviewed, then demanded $5,000 dollars to speak, and finally, after much cajoling and pleading, agreed to sit down without a cash transaction. He said that he demanded money simply to deter journalists who had sought him to discuss Lindh. He considered talking to such people a waste of time and beneath him.

"I don't really care about the money," he explained. "I'm just a moody man."

His emotional self-assessment was an understatement. Virtually humorless, Hayat would turn from indifference to anger in conversation inexplicably and at times grow so frustrated for unclear reasons as to cut off all conversation, only to resume talking moments later with his usual remote demeanor.

His frequent shows of anger made his physique noticeable in a way it wasn't in his quieter moments. He was tall and broad in the shoulders, with an athlete's long waist and legs. Even in his long shalwar qamiz, the traditional pajama-like shirt worn by men and women alike in the region, Hayat's strong frame cut a lean figure.

He became most intense, however, when he took on his missionary role and urged possible converts to embrace Islam. He was an evangelist of the highest zeal and was relentless in his efforts at conversion.

"You will become Muslim," he told me shortly after we met face to face for the first time, saying I must convert to Islam to fully understand all that Lindh underwent.

"One American guy spent a day with me there in America,

and I urged him so much 'become Muslim, become Muslim.' At last he said, 'I will talk with my wife.' Do you have a wife or not?"

When I told him no, he cheered, "Okay, you are a free man!"

Hayat also saw a free man in Lindh, who had many questions about Islam and places to study in Pakistan.

"We had only one day," Hayat said of his first meeting with Lindh in California.

Hayat and several missionary friends were readying to go by road from San Francisco to New York, where they were catching a flight back to Pakistan. On the evening Hayat met Lindh, the group was set to leave San Francisco before dawn the next day. Hayat told Lindh to ride along for the first leg of the road trip and arranged to have a car of Bay Area Muslims follow them so Lindh could return to San Francisco in the second car after Hayat and his Muslim brothers finished talking with him.

"He came with us for about six or seven hours in the car," Hayat said, remembering how he and his fellow Muslim travelers fielded questions from Lindh, who asked about everyday Islamic practices ranging from prayer to Muslim business ethics.

"He had converted two years before, so he just wanted to spend some time talking with Muslim brothers about the religion," Hayat said. "This was the best way since we didn't have much time."

Hayat took the opportunity to describe the Islamic outlook of Tablighi Jamaat, an organization with a following in the millions, dedicated to both spreading Islam and deepening a sense of piety among practicing Muslims.

"Every good thing is Islam, because it is the religion of nature," Hayat said. "What human nature wants, this is Islam. Like human nature wants peace, and to be helpful to everyone. This is all Islam. So I was also talking about this."

Lindh, however, was most interested in learning about Pakistan's madrassas. Lindh told Hayat about his experiences in Yemen, how he was thinking of going abroad someplace else for further studies, and how he wanted to visit Pakistan to see the madrassas firsthand.

"He was in search of a good religious school," Hayat said. "He didn't know about Pakistan at the time. He was just interested in the environment of the madrassa, especially what rules and regulations they have, including whether women were allowed to attend. He took my address and asked me if I would help him if he came to Pakistan. I told him yes."

Hayat gave Lindh his address, but Lindh did not hand over his own as they said their good-byes at a highway rest stop about eight hours east of San Francisco. The group ate and prayed together by the side of the road before the two-car caravan split, with Hayat headed east and Lindh west.

☪

After nine months back home, Lindh eventually finagled another visa and returned to Yemen to resume his Arabic-language studies, not at al-Iman, but at the Center for Arabic Language and Eastern Studies, a school similar to the Yemen Language Center. Lindh was still committed to learning Arabic, although he refused to study at Saleem's school. He might have enrolled at al-Iman, but the school had failed to help him with visa arrangements before and all the classes there were taught at a more advanced level of Arabic than he could grasp. The Center for Arabic Language and Eastern Studies, on the other hand, offered the basic courses Lindh needed at prices that undercut Saleem's school.

The Center for Arabic Language and Eastern Studies sits amid a cluster of minarets deep in the Old City of Sana'a, where the cobblestone roads are joined with dirt alleys roamed by stray cats, loose goats, and the occasional growling dog. The Old City is more conservative religiously than the outer city. Women who fail to cover themselves completely risk angry shouts from men on the street. The alleys are strewn with trash, which gives some bazaars a gutter smell. Like the Yemen Language Center, the Center for Arabic Language and Eastern Studies is a tall walkup stone building. But whereas Saleem keeps his center clean and sunny with modern classroom equipment, Lindh's chosen language school appears dark, cramped, and unkempt with few amenities. Yellowed, curling posters of tourist sites in Yemen hang limply on the walls alongside tacked-up pictures of smiling foreign students. The small, filmy windows have bars. The classrooms are no bigger than a large closet, and most overlook a vacant lot used as a neighborhood dump, as does the sparse reading room and the mafraj.

The founder and headmaster of the Center for Arabic Language and Eastern Studies, Mohammed al-Ansi, apologetically refused an interview, saying he had been instructed to not discuss Lindh by Yemen's shadowy, thuggish political security service, which rebuffed appeals to reconsider the order on al-Ansi as of November 2002.

Jamil al-Bazili, an instructor under al-Ansi who taught Lindh, was only slightly less reticent. Initially, al-Bazili denied knowing Lindh, but recanted when pressed, then spoke haltingly.

"Maybe I taught him some classes, but I don't remember," said al-Bazili, a young Yemeni with short, curly hair and an ashy complexion.

Al-Bazili claimed he had no connection with Lindh outside the classroom and small talk before and afterwards. Lindh was one of about twenty students, mostly from Europe, taking Arabic-language lessons at the time. He didn't stick out, at least to al-Bazili, as he came and went to class.

Former instructor Fari al-Jaradi, however, remembered

Lindh well and spoke at some length, despite fears that he would run afoul of the Yemeni government, Islamic militants, or both. A Yemeni in his mid thirties, al-Jaradi was one of Lindh's favorite instructors, and the two sat together in many private teaching sessions, as Lindh's Arabic outpaced the other students. The two became friends, with Lindh telling al-Jaradi about his troubles at Saleem's center.

"We talked about that," said al-Jaradi, from whose deeply sunned olive face looked two eyes that matched the black of his beard and tussled, stringy hair. "As a Muslim, you know, mixture of male and female students in a class is sometimes unacceptable."

Al-Jaradi would occasionally bring Lindh to his home for family meals and discuss things unrelated to Arabic studies, like al-Jaradi's tour with the mujaheddin in Afghanistan in 1986 and 1987. Lindh, al-Jaradi said, was curious about Afghanistan, but al-Jaradi was reluctant to talk about his jihad with the visiting American student.

"It's something personal," al-Jaradi explained.

Still, al-Jaradi acknowledged that the two talked in some depth about Afghanistan. Al-Jaradi suspected that Lindh was beginning to get ideas about a jihad of his own in Afghanistan, and he tried to wave Lindh off.

"It's not good for him to go there," said al-Jaradi, who urged young Lindh to go back home to his parents.

Lindh had no ideas about returning to California, at least not then. He was set on continuing his overseas studies, and he eventually mastered Arabic enough to sit in on some classes at al-Iman. About five months into his second stay in Yemen, he returned to al-Iman to take more Arabic, as well as courses in Islamic studies. But again he struggled to come up with a long-term visa. Staying in Yemen for any length of time without hassles seemed impossible.

Lindh's difficulties drew his mind back to Pakistan and Khizar Hayat's invitation, which Lindh had not forgotten. Hayat had made a big impression on Lindh, who felt like he really clicked with the Pakistani, despite the short amount of time the two had spent together. In the summer of 2000, Lindh wrote to Hayat, who was by then back in Pakistan studying Islamic law at Peshawar University. In the note, Lindh told Hayat that visa problems still plagued him and that he wished to come to Pakistan to explore the madrassa scene, as they had discussed eight months earlier. Hayat wrote back and told Lindh that he had made the offer to help him find a school in Pakistan with sincerity. Come anytime, Hayat told Lindh. Lindh then called Hayat from Yemen around September 15, 2000, and said he'd be arriving in Islamabad in roughly two weeks.

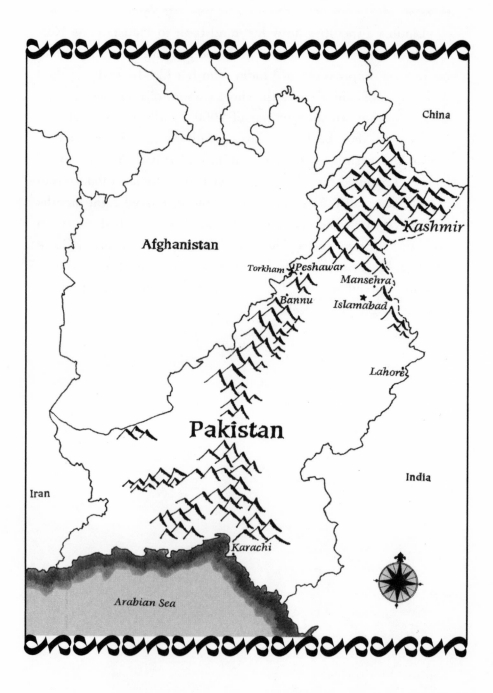

CHAPTER THREE

Purity and Piety on the Northwest Frontier

LINDH'S plane touched down around 2 A.M. on the evening he arrived in Islamabad. At first his luggage didn't seem to have made the trip, and he was forced to search Islamabad's dysfunctional airport for his stuff. Lindh must have looked confused and lost as he tried to sort himself out. Another traveler approached and offered to help find his luggage, and the two spent about an hour together at the airport before resolving everything. Lindh expressed gratitude to the stranger, who identified himself as a Taliban official from Afghanistan. During the brief encounter, the two didn't really do more than search for Lindh's luggage, but the kindness the Talib showed to Lindh left a lasting impression.

Hayat eventually showed up at the airport, as promised, and the two set out for Peshawar, traveling again together, though this time along the darkened stretch of beaten blacktop that leads from Islamabad's ordered boulevards through scenes of easy bedlam in the rocky stretches between the two cities.

On billboards along the way to Peshawar, women with milky faces and black satin hair drink tea and talk into sleek mobile phones while smiling down on the road. As many walkers, loose dogs, and bicyclers as automobiles are on the road making their way through a thin gray dust that blurs headlights. Brightly painted trucks bearing rocks, cattle, wood, potatoes, and chickens jangle with chains hung in ornament and honk like a chorus of off-key trumpets. Covered pickups turned into makeshift buses glide, crammed with travelers, who stand on the bumpers and hang off the back if they can't find a seat on the packed benches under the tarp. Men hunch two by two over tiny motorcycles, threading the slow stream of traffic past idling police at checkpoints who often stop taxis and discreetly demand dollar bribes and free rides.

After about three hours on the road, the traveler approaches Peshawar. The words "Keep Your City Clean" are chalked in English on a bridge at the entrance to the city, whose skyline crowds out the horizon with colorless stacks of concrete buildings draped in thick, yellow smog.

As Hayat drove Lindh onto campus, they would have seen curving slashes of Urdu graffiti, which colors the brick walls around Peshawar University. Urdu uses the same alphabet as Arabic, so Lindh could likely make out the phrases on the walls, which served as a sort of public message board for Islamic militant organizations like Harkat ul Mujaheddin, Lashkar-e-Tayyiba, Jaish-e-Mohammed, and others openly recruiting volunteers willing to fight in Afghanistan and Kashmir.

"Martyrdom Is Your Wish and Ours," reads one message, posted along with a working phone number to the recruiting offices of Hizbul Mujaheddin.

"The Symbol of Heroism, the Afghan Muslim," says another. Still another reads, "Down with the Union of Christians, Jews, and Hindus."

Mujaheddin groups had been using Peshawar as a recruiting hub and way station for Afghanistan since the 1980s. By 2000, when Lindh arrived, many mujaheddin who had fought Russians in Afghanistan were shaping a new generation of Muslim guerrillas who would aid the Taliban's war against the Northern Alliance and wage an insurgency in Indian-held Kashmir. The Pakistani government supported both causes as a matter of national policy, and the banner presence of Islamic militant groups in Peshawar and other cities in Pakistan went unchallenged until after September 11, 2001, despite the appearance of some on the U.S. list of terrorist organizations.

Harkat ul Mujaheddin, the group Lindh would eventually get his first arms training with, painted the phone number to its Peshawar office on a wall near a mosque Lindh visited during his first days in Peshawar, along with a simple message: "Join us to help the mujaheddin fighting in Kashmir and Afghanistan," read the sign; the words "Harkat ul Mujaheddin" or "Movement of Holy Warriors" were painted in ornate Urdu characters big enough for a highway billboard.

If any of the messages stirred Lindh at all then, he didn't mention it to Hayat, who said he made clear that any talk of joining militant movements was unacceptable around him since his role as a Tablighi Jamaat missionary precluded involvement with militant causes.

"He couldn't discuss these things with me, because I told him if you want to find a madrassa I can help you," Hayat said. "Otherwise, you're free."

Lindh stuck with Hayat, who gave him a place to stow his things and a slab of floor to sleep on in a dormitory room Hayat shared with six of his Peshawar University classmates. Over the next several days, Hayat escorted his new American friend through Peshawar's choked streets, adrift with Afghan refugees, many of them wandering women who moaned tearfully beneath their burkas, swishing through Peshawar like ghosts from Afghanistan. Hayat spent time introducing Lindh to fellow Tablighi Jamaat followers and madrassa students around Peshawar. After

☪

a string of largely uneventful days, Hayat and Lindh journeyed to Hayat's family house in Bannu, a hardscrabble desert town about thirty miles east of the Afghan border, deep in Pakistan's lawless Northwest Frontier province.

Gritty mosques and arms bazaars mark the way south from Peshawar through villages with names like Lach, Serai Norvab, and Darra Adam Khel, crumbling hovels of mud walls and corrugated tin roofs knotted together under a snarl of telephone and electrical wires that untangle and stream on deep into the desert. Bannu itself is a dusty maze of shops and houses that look like a one-story storage park overrun by Asian bedouins somewhere out of time. Signs advertising mobile phones, cigarettes, Coca-Cola, and Vicks VapoRub hang over skinned and gutted goats swaying on meat hooks in open air thick with the smell of exhaust, sweat, and animals. Donkey carts clop along, and the occasional wooly camel lopes through a chaotic swirl of traffic where rickshaws, Chinese bicycles resembling vintage Schwinns, and shiny new Japanese autos lurch and honk. In doorways and on sidewalks, men in turbans, prayer caps, baseball hats, and the distinctive oversized wooly berets called pakols sit passively, squatting on their haunches, or lay on rope cots in a haze buzzing with the hum of flies flitting over rickety wheel carts piled with withered fruit and vegetables.

Hayat put Lindh up in his parents' house and showed him around Bannu, where all the locals they met offered him a warm welcome. Bannu's arid destitution mattered little to Lindh, who mingled easily with Hayat's family and village friends. He and his host began discussing where he would find a school for memorizing the Koran, a pursuit seen by many Muslim scholars as a prerequisite for higher study of Islam. Lindh had already made some progress in memorizing the Koran during his time in Yemen, but faced a daunting prospect nonetheless. Both Hayat and Lindh felt that a quiet, comfortable school would be the best place. Hayat had some ideas about where Lindh should go, but the school search had to be put off initially because Hayat was due in Lahore for a Tablighi Jamaat conference. Hayat took Lindh along, showing his young American friend some of Pakistan's sights.

When they returned to Bannu, Hayat and Lindh focused on finding a madrassa. Hayat felt that Lindh should see the biggest institutions in Pakistan because they were most likely to have accommodations and programs for foreign students, whereas the tiny rural madrassas were not. Hayat thought Lindh might do well at places like the Jamia Ahrasia madrassa in Lahore or one of the many Karachi madrassas such as Daral Uloom, Ashraf ul Maddaris, and Jamia Binuria. Hayat mapped out a five-day madrassa tour, and the two set out, traveling in buses and taxis to a host of schools under consideration. Neither Lindh nor Hayat was particularly loquacious, so they talked little along the way. Moreover, what little English Hayat had picked up in America was quickly escaping him, leaving them struggling to understand each other much of the time. Hayat tried, nonetheless, to teach Lindh about Pakistan.

Hayat explained how a mix of no less than six distinct ethnic groups, each with its own unique language and traditions, populated Pakistan's four provinces. Hayat told Lindh about the differences between people like the Punjabis, the majority in Pakistan, and the Pashtuns, whose tribal society ruled the area along the border with Afghanistan. Hayat also complained and alternately apologized to Lindh about the everyday problems in Pakistani society that cut across local cultures, like unreliable transportation, pollution, poverty, the masses of Afghan refugees living in squalor, and the urban underdevelopment that left running water and electricity uncertain in parts of even major cities.

"I took him as a guest so I had to take care of him," Hayat said, adding that he worried whether some of the grimmer third-world scenes and experiences of Pakistan alienated Lindh. "I asked him, 'How do you feel in Pakistan?'"

"I feel very good here," Lindh replied.

Lindh appeared altogether unconcerned with the colors, sights, sounds, and tastes of Pakistan, good and bad alike. He just wanted to find someplace quiet where he could memorize the Koran.

"He didn't care about the beauty or other worldly things," Hayat said. "He cared only about the religious schools and his religion."

Lindh withheld judgment on each institution he saw as they traveled, telling Hayat he would weigh one against the other only after visiting as many as possible.

"I will see all the madrassas, then I will decide something," Lindh told him.

Lindh didn't see any schools that he liked during the road trip with Hayat, and he returned to Bannu undecided about what to do. Hayat was at a loss. He had shown Lindh just about every-place he could think of in Pakistan. If none of the best schools in Pakistan's biggest cities appealed to Lindh, what would?

C

Mufti Mohammed Iltimas Khan first met Lindh in the fall of 2000 at a mosque on the outskirts of Bannu. Lindh had come for prayers with Hayat, whom Iltimas first met by chance in 1989 in Rawalpindi, near Islamabad, despite their common hometown, Bannu. In 1989, both Hayat and Iltimas were committed Islamic scholars exploring schools throughout Pakistan, and they stayed in close touch after quickly bonding over their similar religious studies and upbringing. Around Bannu, Iltimas saw Hayat about once every week or two, so it was no surprise to find him at prayer the day he brought Lindh.

"Ahhh, the first time I met him was in Bannu," Iltimas said, remembering aloud in his gravelly voice how he saw Lindh with Hayat.

"I asked my friend, 'Khizar Hayat, who is the person with you?'" said Iltimas, whose apple cheeks pinched his still, brown eyes deeply into his bearded face whenever he smiled and laughed, as he often did. "He's not Pakistani. He told me, 'Yes sir, he's from America and also he was in Yemen, and he came from Yemen here to visit me. He wishes to memorize the Holy Koran.'"

Within minutes of Hayat's introductions, Lindh announced that he wanted to enroll in Iltimas's madrassa, which Hayat had previously mentioned to Lindh. Iltimas tried to stop him from making a hasty decision about settling there and told Lindh he should at least see the place before making a commitment to enroll.

"I told him no, Suleyman, first you come here to learn about the procedure of studying and memorizing and also the place and also about eating and some other things, the traditions," Iltimas said. "After that you should decide about staying with me."

Like most others, Iltimas's madrassa is spartan and remote, tucked into an outlying village of Bannu named Hassani Kalan Surani. From a dusty alley carved deep into Hassani Kalan Surani, beside a fork of date trees, two dented metal doors painted blue open into Iltimas's madrassa, which appears at first glance to be still under construction. A pile of loose bricks leans against the outside wall next to a cluttered heap of empty paint buckets, overturned rope beds, a wooden bench, and an unused ladder made of rough-hewn wooden poles. The dusty jumble faces the shaded windows of Iltimas's corner study, adjacent to a storage room, a tiny makeshift kitchen, and a small prayer hall under the madrassa's shallow breezeway. Iltimas's study, where Lindh sometimes slept, is bare except for a corner table holding the madrassa's only phone, a locked book cupboard mounted on the wall, and a set of shelves standing over the suitcase of personal items Lindh left behind.

As Iltimas and I sat on the floor of the study in the spring of 2002, talking and drinking tea with buffalo milk, the sound of boys chanting Koran verses in the hall hummed through walls thickened with layer over layer of white paint hopelessly grimed by desert dust. Occasionally, one of the younger boys would peal into long, high wails above the others for a few verses, carrying the chorus of chants sharply into the mosque's courtyard over bricks worn smooth by the dust ground into them under worshipers' knees. When the steady chants fell off as students broke between lessons, the only sounds in the hush of the madrassa were the faucets dripping into mossy drains and the buzzing of flies, which flit off drying laundry and pillbox prayer caps hung on wall pegs. Here was the quiet place Lindh had sought. To an outsider, the madrassa's dingy austerity might be off-putting. But Lindh saw everything he wanted within the tiny school's four walls: a bed, space to pray, and a peaceful place to read.

Iltimas possessed a warm and friendly nature, and he often laughed at himself when struggling in his serviceable English to name things like "sleeping bag" and "envelope." His laugh was contagious, often drawing others around him into long bouts of chuckles over inane things. As head of the madrassa, Iltimas played the gentle master, calling for meals and tea from his students with a murmur and wave of his hand and ignoring the boys as they set plates before him and cleared them away. Iltimas's students remained stiff and silent around him, though without a hint of fear. Whenever they served us as we talked, they made quick

work of it and then moved quietly to the corners of the room before drifting off together without a word.

Iltimas was clearly intelligent, fluent in Arabic and for the
most part English. He was, of course, steeped in Islamic scholarly
knowledge, having memorized the entire Koran himself. But unlike some myopic religious instructors, Iltimas had read widely of
works outside Islam and enjoyed discussing things like World
War II and the 1947 partition of British India. However, underneath the warmth and outward graces, Iltimas held fast to a core
of fundamentalist Islamic beliefs in step with the ethos of the Taliban and other militant Muslim movements. He would quickly
shed his humor and his face would darken when he was chal-
lenged on any point related to his particular views on politics, history, religion, and other matters.

In his early thirties, Iltimas wore a tightly wrapped, powder
blue turban and carried a bulging potbelly in his shalwar qamiz.
The weight in his stomach seemed to anchor him like a swallowed
bowling ball while he shifted and rocked on the floor of his study,
recounting his earliest days with Lindh.

Iltimas saw Lindh again a few days after their first encounter
when Hayat brought him to tour the madrassa. Lindh's mind already seemed set on staying as Iltimas led him around the modest
grounds. "They came and he saw the place and the procedure of
studying and memorizing, then he decided," Iltimas said. "After
two or three days he brought his things." Iltimas remembered
Lindh fondly. He kept his absent student's things carefully stored
in his study, saying he would send them back to Lindh or his family if ever asked. "He was sweet," Iltimas said of Lindh. "Khizar
[Hayat] told me he was a good-minded, quiet man, sincere
toward Islam and not one to get involved in other affairs."

Iltimas said he thought that Lindh felt comfortable with him
and wanted to begin studies right away because they could com-

municate in English and Arabic, which helped Lindh overcome his inability to speak Pashto or Urdu, the most commonly spoken languages in Pakistan. Iltimas also said he thought that Hayat had strongly recommended his madrassa, although Hayat struggled to remember this fact, stressing that he had forgotten much of the details of his time with Lindh.

Iltimas seemed unconcerned about Lindh's reasons and means, in any case. He never asked Lindh for money and never troubled him for any expectable prerequisites, like proof of a student visa, transcripts, or letters of recommendation, a school policy Lindh likely found appealing after his experiences in Yemen. Iltimas simply took Lindh in when Hayat brought him and his things to the madrassa on November 30, 2000.

"He was my guest like you are my guest. If you stay here, I am ready for you," he told me. "This is our tradition."

The welcome Iltimas showed Lindh was nothing unusual. Customary Islamic hospitality calls for Muslims to host visiting travelers with generosity, and Iltimas offered charity to outsiders at his madrassa long before Lindh ever came. Iltimas opens his madrassa to anyone in Hassani Kalan Surani, and a trickle of villagers comes and goes throughout the day. Some of the village children who aren't enrolled still attend afternoon lessons and prayers before going home at night, while the full-time pupils stay at the mosque, sleeping on the floor's curling blue carpet under rickety fans. Adults, especially older villagers, drift in regularly to answer the azzan that Iltimas or one of his select students voices five times a day through a tangle of battered megaphones strung with drooping cords atop one of the madrassa's four stubby minarets.

Iltimas seemed perfectly content overseeing his squat madrassa, which he opened in 1996 with help from a Kuwaiti nongovernmental organization called Lagnat-ul-Dawa al Islamia Kuwait, one of several religious charities that have long funneled money from the Middle East to start up Islamic schools in Muslim communities outside the Arab world. With the Kuwaiti seed money, Iltimas threw up four concrete walls around the small rooms, a courtyard, and the prayer hall and called the grounds Abdurehman Abdullah Mohammad, adding his miniature Islamic institution to the scores of others like it that flourish throughout Pakistan, especially in the tribal areas.

Tens of thousands of such unregulated schools have sprung up in the absence of an effective educational system in Pakistan, where only about two out of every five adults can read, a literacy rate behind even most other developing countries. Unlike many isolated areas of Pakistan, Bannu has a working public school that gives parents an option in choosing their children's education. But madrassas like Iltimas's still draw young pupils, whose families often see the intensive religious curriculum as a disciplined Islamic piety ill taught in classes funded by the government. While Pakistani public schools offer a broad range of academic subjects, most madrassas narrowly focus on religious instruction.

Iltimas's madrassa housed roughly forty boys aged ten to seventeen. The core curriculum revolved around memorization of the Koran. Lindh and his fellow students followed a rigorous routine, despite the overall atmosphere of serenity at the madrassa. Iltimas wakes his students before dawn for ablutions and the early prayer and then gathers them in the main hall to open their Korans for readings that last until sunrise. After a short breakfast, Iltimas and the class return to lessons that last until noon, when they break again for prayer and a two-hour lunch. More readings follow the midday break, and the students recite and memorize with Iltimas or his designated substitute until the third call to prayer late in the afternoon. Readings and exercises continue until the fourth call, which comes at dusk. The students do the last of their lessons as the sun lowers and close their Korans for the day at the fifth and final call to prayer.

During lessons in the prayer hall, students sit on the floor in a semicircle around their teacher, who rests on a cushion with his back to a wall lined with the madrassa's library of Korans. The room remains dim, even with a bright midday sun outside. At night, naked fluorescent bulbs hung high on the bare walls glow milky green. Lindh, as the elder student, sat directly to the teacher's right with the rest of the boys positioned in order from oldest to youngest going counterclockwise around the circle. All of the students don pillbox prayer caps during lessons and prop their Korans on tiny book stools called raheels, so that the holy book never touches the floor. They rock as they chant, each student sonorously swaying to rhythms of the verses in his particular readings. They dip to press their faces close to the pages and reel backward into ululating exclamations of holy verse, weaving their voices fluidly and harmoniously in hypnotic overlapping passages.

"It is a spiritual procedure," Iltimas said of the rocking and chanting, which supposedly allows students to achieve a sort of meditative trance, blocking out everything but the words of the Koran. Lindh himself initially sat rigid during his lessons, moving only his mouth as he recited. Iltimas urged Lindh to loosen up. Lindh did, somewhat, occasionally rocking stiffly in tiny sways that appeared hardly noticeable alongside the near gymnastic readings of some of his schoolmates. Iltimas knows exactly where each of his pupils is in his lessons by listening carefully to students one by one as they read and chant.

"The teacher knows the mind of every student," Iltimas said, adding that the relationship between student and teacher "needs to be close for spiritual education."

Lindh spent many afternoons and evenings simply sitting with

Iltimas in the mufti's study, where they lounged on the floor drinking tea and chatting. As always with Lindh, his talks focused primarily on questions concerning Islam. Iltimas was vocal about a wider array of subjects, and he would often go off on long-winded opinions about history, current events, or whatever else was on his mind, while Lindh listened passively. At times, Iltimas lectured Lindh as a teacher and spiritual mentor, taking on the airs of a wizened dean. Lindh showed Iltimas due respect as a host and a friend, but regarded him more as an overly opinionated groundskeeper at the madrassa than as his instructor. Lindh knew the places to go for serious religious studies were the Muslim universities in the Middle East, not the badlands of Pakistan, where rambling muftis hold village courts. Iltimas, to Lindh, offered a place to memorize the Koran before furthering his formal Islamic education elsewhere, so he politely and quietly endured Iltimas's sermons and questions as part of his unusual residency.

As the only foreign student, Lindh quickly took on a celebrity status, spending much more time with Iltimas than any of the other pupils. Everything was taken care of for Lindh at Iltimas's madrassa, including his meals and laundry. The mufti even offered to buy things for Lindh whenever they went to the Bannu bazaar together, small everyday stuff. But Lindh used his own money to pay for things like soap and souvenirs.

"He was our guest student," Iltimas said of Lindh, describing him as a sort of American scholar in residence at his tiny school, a symbol of the American students he had never had a chance to know. In 1997, the mufti had seriously considered traveling to the United States like Hayat had, but he didn't pursue the idea because he thought there would be too many restrictions on his teachings. "I chose to stay in Bannu, but Allah sent an American student to me anyway," Iltimas told me. "I used to ask questions about America, what type of civilization Americans have. I was far away from America, and he was near to us and near to them."

"I used to ask questions like that, about his past life and other things, but he didn't tell me anything about it," Iltimas recalled. "One day he told me about his parents separation. I asked him, do they live together? After that he explained." But Iltimas added that what Lindh told him was strictly "a secret for me."

Lindh told Iltimas virtually nothing about his childhood and very little about his time in Yemen. Overall, Lindh seemed happy to put aside his past in America and recent troubles in Yemen in order to focus on his life and studies in Pakistan.

"He was most satisfied," said Iltimas.

Iltimas remembered Lindh longing for family only once, when he said he had been missing his younger sister, Naomi, during Eid, the Muslim holiday that marks the close of the Islamic holy month of Ramadan.

Lindh was still staying in touch with his family and friends in San Francisco via e-mail. He frequented an Internet club in Bannu nearly every day before he enrolled in Iltimas's madrassa. But after taking up his studies, Lindh began sending e-mails less frequently, usually about once a week or so. One day at the Internet club, Iltimas peered over Lindh's shoulder and grinned when he saw how the boy addressed his mother. "Mama?" the mufti said, gently teasing Lindh.

Iltimas wasn't the only one who occasionally peeked at Lindh's electronic missives home. Akhtar Khan, who has a shop in the Bannu bazaar near the small dry goods store kept by Hayat's family, said he used to go with Lindh to send e-mail when Lindh appeared for his regular visits to Hayat.

"One time I was at an Internet club with Suleyman. . . . A man who speaks English looked over Suleyman's shoulder as he was writing," said Khan, a rotund man, mostly bald save a graying curl of hair around the crown of his head that matched his pointed beard. "He said he was writing to his mother about Islam and urging her to become a Muslim too."

Lindh sent e-mails to his mother often. On December 3, 2000, he dropped her a note making fun of recently elected President George W. Bush, calling him "your new President." And he added, "I'm glad he's not mine." In later notes home, Lindh expressed an increasingly dim view of the United States and the West. He wrote to his mother on February 8, 2001, saying, "I don't really want to see America again." Lindh's mother naturally urged him to come home for a visit nonetheless. But Lindh wrote on March 1, 2001, that he was "busy in my studies and I have no intention of interrupting them for any reason in the near future. When I went to Yemen the first time, you demanded my return before I was able to complete my goal of learning Arabic. After returning, I wasted about 9 months in America in which I achieved nothing and forgot much of what I had learned while in Yemen."

Lindh's familiarity with e-mail and computers in general meant he was one of the few people around Bannu who knew anything about the machines. So when the madrassa doctor's computer broke, he brought it to Lindh at Iltimas's madrassa, where Iltimas and Lindh were having lunch in the study.

Lindh plugged the machine in, booted it up, and licked his fingers as he continued to eat while pecking away at the keyboard to work out the glitch. The ease with which his student fixed a computer impressed Iltimas.

"Suleyman, I want to learn about computers," he recalled saying to Lindh. "Will you teach me?" But Lindh told him, "It's a waste of time."

Lindh apparently thought time was more valuably spent in pursuit of Islam. Always the diligent student, he made steady progress in his efforts to memorize the Koran, studying twelve hours a day.

"He was attentive to his studies all the time," Iltimas said. "He was intent on memorizing the Holy Koran. He was always asking me, in how many years and in how many months will I remember the Holy Koran. He was very concerned. After two months he was asking me."

After a couple of months, when Iltimas felt Lindh had made enough progress in his studies, the mufti asked his special pupil to step to the loudspeaker and voice the Isha, the fifth and final azzan of the day.

At first Lindh demurred, but Iltimas insisted.

"Suleyman, it's time," he told Lindh.

The azzan expresses Islam's essence in the shortest possible phrases voiced in a solemn melody that sounds more like singing than chanting to someone who's never heard it before. Reluctantly, Lindh unhitched the mouthpiece and chanted the Arabic, floating his voice in scratchy metallic echoes into the chorus of azzan rising from the other mosques and madrassas scattered over the darkened rocky plains stretching toward Afghanistan.

"Allah is great, Allah is great, Allah is great, Allah is great," Lindh intoned in Arabic. "There is no god but Allah, there is no god but Allah. Mohammed is the prophet of Allah, Mohammed is the prophet of Allah. Come to prayer, come to prayer. Come for salvation, come for salvation. Allah is great. Allah is great. There is no god but Allah."

As he seemed to be quickly advancing in his religious studies, Lindh began to have vague ideas for future plans. Lindh expressed his ultimate hope of becoming an Islamic teacher in America after furthering his education in Pakistan. He considered enrolling in formal Islamic studies in the Northwest Frontier province, but worried about his lack of Urdu or Pashto and asked Iltimas about the possibility of taking courses in Pakistan, despite the language barrier. "I said yes, it's possible," Iltimas said. "There are some madrassas that teach in Arabic and Urdu."

According to Iltimas, Lindh eventually confided that the prevailing gender mores provided part of his reason for his wanting to remain in the area. Local custom mandated burkas for women whenever they left their homes, which occurred rarely, as in Taliban Afghanistan. Though Lindh saw no room for women in his life during school days, he hoped to enjoy female companionship at some point. Lindh told Iltimas he eventually planned to take four wives, the maximum number allowed for Muslims.

"He asked me the second or the third night if I were alone here," Iltimas recalled laughingly, baring teeth stained by countless cups of tea and squirming with an adolescent's giddy embarrassment at talk of girls. "I told him yes, I am unmarried. I asked him, Suleyman, how many marriages will you have? He told me four!"

During one of their many hours of conversation, Lindh told Iltimas how after converting to Islam he began to feel uncomfortable living in the United States and became naturally drawn to Islamic countries, where his adopted faith played a part in everyday society.

Lindh told Iltimas that he felt as though he could neither explore his newfound religion deeply nor live by the commands of Islamic scripture properly in his native country, where he saw many societal ills. Lindh told Iltimas that a widespread misconception about America hid things like the brimming jails, soaring crime rates, and other troubling trends.

"Only a positive picture is given to the world, not the negative," Iltimas said. "He was fed up with American society. He was searching for a place where people follow and obey all the commands of Allah. America was not suitable for this."

Iltimas agreed, often pointing to the Monica Lewinsky scandal as a sign of America's moral decay.

"If in a country like America a girl is not safe at the hands of the head of state, then how can a common man ever feel secure?" Iltimas said. "If the head of state is telling lies and doing such things, then what does that say about the common people of the society, the public at large?"

Iltimas seemed transfixed by the Monica Lewinsky scandal and often ranted about the affair to Lindh, who really couldn't care less and wondered why this mufti in Pakistan seemed so absorbed by it. Lindh disregarded the scandal and talked more about larger political issues, also voicing his disenchantment with certain Islamic societies.

"He didn't like the present setup of Muslim governments," Iltimas said. "He used to say Muslim governments were in the hands of the West and America. He wanted an Islam like it was in its earliest days, free of influence by America and other outside powers."

Iltimas likewise held strong opinions about that and other issues. Like many others in Bannu, Iltimas had a strong affinity for the Taliban, and he often told Lindh how he felt about Afghanistan, as he did with so many other things on his mind.

"I used to express my feelings and opinions in front of him," Iltimas said.

Iltimas saw the Islamic militia as the truest bearers of Islam. Lindh heard the voice of the Taliban frequently through Iltimas, who often listened to a small transistor radio tuned to Radio Shariat, the Taliban station that broadcast propaganda and Taliban edicts from Kabul.

"Freedom radio without any music," Iltimas said of Radio Shariat. "Music is prohibited in Islam."

Iltimas smiled as he remembered Lindh asking him what he was listening to so intently when the radio voices from Taliban Kabul crackled in Iltimas's hand. Iltimas would listen carefully to the Radio Shariat broadcasts whenever Lindh was around and then translate for his student.

Before the Taliban lost power late in 2001, Radio Shariat broadcast readings of the Taliban's interpretation of Islamic law, which included decrees outlawing, among other things, all forms of art, which the Taliban saw as idolatry. The Taliban ideologues viewed virtually every element of human behavior as subject to stringent Islamic laws, which they twisted into perversions religiously unrecognizable to Muslims outside the radical school of fundamentalism taught in scores of madrassas by the likes of Iltimas.

"They were true Muslims," Iltimas said wistfully of the Taliban, a movement whose ranks from the earliest days in 1994 had been flush with vigilante students educated in Pakistani madrassas.

Many prominent Muslim thinkers regarded the Taliban's fight against the Northern Alliance in the nineties as merely unfinished business of the eighties. The Taliban, its backers thought, were fighting to establish a pure Islamic state against a renegade Muslim group, the Northern Alliance. Many viewed the Alliance as a puppet of modern Russia because of its financial backing by former Soviet republics, such as Tajikistan. The reality of the situation was more complex.

Ahmed Shah Massoud, a commander even Abdullah Azzam pointed to as the most brilliant fighter against the Soviets, led the Northern Alliance. As a Muslim and a holy warrior, he possessed impeccable credentials. The war between the Taliban and the Northern Alliance had more to do with the ethnic divisions in Afghanistan than with religious struggle. Pashtun tribesmen dominated the Taliban's forces and leadership, whereas Tajiks and Uzbeks filled the Northern Alliance ranks. Moreover, the Taliban's pure Islamic state was a tragic joke.

After the Taliban seized the Afghan capital, Kabul, in 1996, their notorious draconian Islamic law included a virtual ban on females in public and mandatory beards for men. Any man without a beard was to be jailed until his facial hair grew in to an appropriately "bushy" length. Any woman seen in public risked a beating from the feared Taliban religious police if she were not properly covered. Flying kites was banned, as was keeping birds as pets and dozens of other simple activities of everyday life that easily passed as normal, acceptable behavior for men and women in Western and Islamic societies alike.

As a government, the Taliban amounted to little more than a militia ruling with martial law over desolate lands shattered by war. Most Islamic leaders and educated thinkers took the Taliban's one-eyed spiritual leader, Mullah Mohammed Omar, about as seriously as a carnival mystic. Only three nations, Pakistan, the United Arab Emirates, and Saudi Arabia, recognized the Taliban as the rightful government of Afghanistan. Even certain members of the al-Qaida leadership, living as honored guests of the Taliban, saw their hosts as uneducated, backward country bumpkins, easily manipulated with religious appeals.

Iltimas rejected out of hand the near universal condemnation of the Taliban voiced up to and after September 11 by Western and Islamic countries alike. He said those who questioned the Taliban's brand of Islamic governance, the harshest ever seen in the history of Islam, were either misguided Muslims or Western demagogues bent on subverting Afghanistan and the wider Islamic world, an argument the Taliban itself sounded throughout its rule.

Iltimas said that initially Lindh's curiosity about Afghanistan seemed like a passing interest. "Sometimes he asked me about Afghanistan," Iltimas said. "As a common person, during eating and taking tea."

But Lindh's interest grew, and soon he began reading books about the Taliban in his free time, including poetry extolling the

Taliban's rise to power. Iltimas grinned and nodded when I asked him if he had seen Lindh reading Taliban books, which he insisted that he did not give him. Iltimas did admit to showing Lindh a pro-Taliban newspaper printed weekly in English, though.

By and by, Lindh became increasingly convinced that the Taliban's Afghanistan embodied Islamic society in its purest form, a modern representation of the era of the prophet that began on the Arabian Peninsula in A.D. 610 with Mohammed's revelations near Mecca. The Taliban claimed they were shaping a society as such—a pure Islamic state to lead the rest of the Muslim world, which they saw as adrift in Western corruption.

"He thought of the Taliban as the ideal model for Islam for the twenty-first century, a Muslim movement that would end the societal ills he saw in America and elsewhere," Iltimas said. "The country of Afghanistan at the time of the Taliban, he was searching for such a place."

Lindh began to act out some of the Taliban's creeds, showing scorn for things like art that were legal in Pakistan, but banned just across the border. He scratched off any pictures on the pads he used to jot down notes about Islamic histories, Arabic translations, or vocabulary terms of Pashto. One notebook Lindh left behind with Iltimas had a drawing of a herd of galloping horses on the cover. Lindh had blackened out the faces of the horses with a marker and tore at the bodies with deep, looping scratches of a pen.

While Lindh began to identify more and more with the Taliban religiously and politically, Afghanistan wasn't the only Muslim land on his mind. He and Iltimas also discussed Islamic issues as they related to places like Bosnia, the Philippines, and India, where Iltimas said the Hindu majority egregiously oppressed and victimized the Muslim minority.

"Sometimes he discussed Bosnia, and also the Philippines,

sometimes," Iltimas said. "Sometimes he discussed Muslims in some countries. But he was not, and I was also not, interested in speaking about those people. I told him the Muslims there in India, that is the problem for me. I always tried to move his mind toward the Muslims in India. The British rulers divided Muslims. Some Muslims are there in the cage of Bangladesh, some Muslims are in the cage of Pakistan. And some Muslims are there in India. . . . Some Muslims are there in the cage of Kashmir."

Talk of Kashmir angered Iltimas like no other subject, and he grew visibly agitated when discussing the troubled region nearby. Kashmir upset Iltimas so much that he tried to avoid talking about it even with Lindh. The issue incensed him, as it does many deeply religious Muslims in Pakistan, and he didn't want to brood over it in the company of guests. But sometimes the mufti just couldn't help himself. Iltimas told Lindh about regional history, explaining in his own way the legacy of the East India Company, the era of the Raj, and the 1947 partition of British India that simultaneously created the states of India and Pakistan, sparking a series of border wars in the region fought largely along religious lines between Hindus and Muslims. Chief among the conflicts was the disputed Himalayan territory known as Kashmir, a predominantly Muslim border area claimed by both India and Pakistan.

During the 1947 partition of the British colonial holdings, the Hindu ruler of Kashmir waffled in his choice of whether to accede his Muslim-dominated state to Pakistan or India. After Islamic fighters from Pakistan's Northwest Frontier province tried to force his hand by infiltrating Kashmir, he made a deal, whereby Kashmir would join the new Indian state, in return for protection by Indian forces. War broke out, and the ensuing peace deal brokered by the United Nations called for a plebiscite so the inhabitants of Kashmir could decide their own fate. However, a plebiscite was never held, and low-level insurgencies, occasionally blossoming into full-blown war, have plagued the region ever since.

Kashmir remains a galvanizing war cry for Pakistani Muslims, who feel the Kashmiris should join with their Islamic brethren in Pakistan, rather than fall under the control of the avowedly secular government of India. The fact that a referendum was never held adds to the feelings of grave injustice among Muslims in the region.

In the early 1990s, the picturesque mountain region became the scene of an open insurgency driven by Islamic militants from Pakistan that would claim some 35,000 lives by 2002. In response to the uprising, the Indian government enacted security legislation in Kashmir, which broadly expanded powers of detention and arrest. Rampant abuse of their new-found power by members of Indian security forces led to claims by Muslim civilians of arbitrary arrest and detention, torture, rape, and extrajudicial executions. While many of the claims do have validity, the suffering of Kashmiri Muslims has been exaggerated by Islamic militants seeking to expand their base of support in Pakistan and elsewhere around the world. Groups such as the Harkat ul Mujaheddin display pictures of brutalized Kashmiri children in their recruitment drives for jihad.

Lindh obviously paid attention to the available reports on the suffering of the Kashmiri people, as an entry in his notebook outlined points related to an article he had recently read. At the top of the page, Lindh wrote "Kashmir" in block letters, numbering seven points below, each one a war statistic he had taken from Islamic fundamentalist literature widely available in Pakistan. By Lindh's count, in the years spanning 1991 to 1999 some "60,000 Kashmiris have been killed," with another "26,000 wounded." He was convinced there were "461 school children burned alive" in the same period and that "700 women between ages of 7 and 70 have been raped." Still more, Lindh cited "39,000 disabled for life" and another "97,000 missing," with "47,000 forced from their homes."

The figures Lindh read about Kashmir were just some of the widely printed stories that appear daily in Pakistan's press, which has many English newspapers of dubious veracity that readily air government propaganda about the issue. All the articles telling of tragedies in Kashmir, as well as the things Lindh heard by word of mouth from Pakistanis, began to weigh more heavily on his mind.

Bosnia, the Philippines, Chechnya, and other conflict zones with Muslims at war were far away from Bannu. Kashmir was just a day's drive, and the idea of Muslims suffering so close began to rouse Lindh, who wondered aloud to Iltimas and Hayat why more Muslims were not coming to the aid of the Kashmiris. Was it not an obligation to aid Muslims in need at a time of war, as Azzam argued?

In Azzam's time, Afghanistan had offered the most valiant cause for jihad, and indeed thousands of Muslims, including Americans, answered the call. In the 1980s, uncounted scores of American jihadis traveled to Afghanistan to fight against the Soviet occupation, a war effort financially backed by the Reagan administration. The trend continued through the 1990s, although Afghanistan became but one of several other destinations for jihadis. Figures are sketchy, since U.S. authorities do not track the overseas travels of American citizens. Terrorism experts at the Federal Bureau of Investigation have estimated that up to 2,000 Muslim Americans left the United States during the 1990s to fight in places like Bosnia, Chechnya, Afghanistan, and Kashmir. In Pakistan, authorities put the number of Americans jihadis believed to have trained in either Pakistan or Afghanistan since

1989 at around 400. Before September 11, the trend raised little concern among U.S. officials, who remained lax about enforcing laws prohibiting U.S. citizens from taking up arms against countries at peace with America. And the number of American jihadis, though ever growing, represented a tiny fraction of the estimated eight million Muslims in America.

Iltimas and Hayat, as followers of Tablighi Jamaat, didn't feel they should play a role in jihadi causes—and they didn't feel that Lindh should either. In conversations with Lindh, both Iltimas and Hayat agreed in principle with Azzam's teachings, that Muslims were obligated to go on jihad, if able, to assist the nearest Muslims in need. Lindh began to wonder what everyone was doing sitting around in Bannu then. Why had Hayat and Iltimas not gone to aid the Muslims in Kashmir? Why shouldn't he go? Iltimas and Hayat told Lindh to forget about it and instead concentrate on memorizing the Koran. Jihad was not a concern for teachers and students, their thinking went. Lindh let it go, for a time.

Lindh began to find it hard to concentrate on his studies as months wore on. He found himself dwelling on Kashmir, when he should have been focused on verses of the Koran. The ethic of jihad as Azzam had explained it in the writings Lindh had read was now becoming a matter of conscience for Lindh, who saw no reason why he himself should not be obliged to fight for the ummah. Lindh was beginning to feel like a hypocrite for not getting involved in some way. In *Join the Caravan*, Azzam writes:

> What is the matter with the students that they do not take a year off from their studies in order to attain the distinction of jihad, and contribute with their own selves to the establishment of Allah's religion on earth? . . . What is the matter with the imams, that they do not sincerely advise those who seek counsel from them regarding

going out with blood and soul in the Path of Allah? For how long will the believing youths be held back and restrained from jihad? These youths, whose hearts are burning with a fire, spurting forth enthusiasm, and blazing with zeal that their pure blood may irrigate the earth of the Muslims. The one who forbids a young man from jihad is no different from the one who forbids him from prayer and fasting.

Lindh had a running debate with both Iltimas and Hayat about such questions, but their answer always remained the same. Hayat was an active member of Tablighi Jamaat and therefore forbidden to get involved in anything like jihad. While not officially an activist, Iltimas agreed with Tablighi Jamaat's ethos, despite his empathy for the Taliban and the Muslims of India, Kashmir, and other troubled lands. "I'm not a warrior, I'm a teacher," Iltimas said. "Khizar is also a teacher."

Lindh disagreed. He felt an obligation to undertake jihad, even if Hayat and Iltimas would not. Being in San Francisco or even Yemen was one thing when considering a Muslim's obligation for jihad, Lindh thought. But there he was in Pakistan, close enough to go, with nothing to stop him. He continued to press Hayat on the matter, knowing Hayat could likely introduce him to people in Peshawar who would be willing to give him arms training. Hayat resisted still, managing to persuade Lindh to remain in Bannu until the spring of 2001, when the desert's cool, dry days began to lengthen and grow hotter in prelude to brutal summer weather.

Lindh eventually told Iltimas that he wanted to take a leave from his studies in cooler climes to avoid Bannu's summer heat. Iltimas discussed the idea with Hayat and agreed to let Lindh go in May. In what looks like his last e-mail home, Lindh wrote to his mother on April 27, 2001, saying that he was going to "some cold mountainous region."

Lindh hardly packed anything. He took only a backpack and sleeping bag with him the day he left, leaving a full suitcase and his burgeoning library of books on Islam with Iltimas for safe-keeping. Lindh didn't say when he'd be back, though.

"You're leaving, but your things are still here. When will you return?" Iltimas recalled asking Lindh in the doorway of the study as they said goodbye. Lindh shrugged and smiled, but did not answer. He thought at the time that he might be gone for a couple of months before coming back to Bannu to pick up his things, then returning to California to visit his family. He thought he would probably be back in the United States by Christmas 2001.

As Lindh was leaving, Iltimas asked him to sign a journal he kept in the study that served as sort of a guest book and message pad. Lindh wrote a simple entry in Arabic, penning his name as Suleyman al-Faris alongside the dates he had studied with Iltimas and the number of Koran sections he had memorized, which accounted for roughly a third of the holy book. Then he wrote another entry just below in English that made Iltimas smile whenever he reread it: "I am Suleyman Lindh," the boy wrote. "Eater of much wheat crop, drinker of much buffalo tea."

Iltimas walked Lindh from the study and through the yard to the alley, where Khizar Hayat waited on his tiny Honda motorcycle, with an engine hardly bigger than a lawnmower's. Iltimas and Lindh had already said their personal goodbyes inside, so they exchanged few final words as Lindh climbed onto the bike. Hayat wheeled the motorcycle around and drove them both through the dust of the alley and out towards Peshawar, traveling together yet again, hunched over Hayat's Honda as they bounced over the potted tracks out of town. It was the last time Iltimas saw Lindh in person.

CHAPTER FOUR

Answering the Call to Arms

FROM Bannu, a smooth blacktop road twistingly opens scenes of planes and mountains in shifting desert hues, patched here and there with tidy green fields, where lonely figures in earth-colored shawls walk through rows of wheat. The wooden faces of men who watch travelers pass reflect the stillness in the air dotted with tattered kites that dart and wobble in search of breezes. Circles of children scamper in giggles. Sunlight gleams off the colored beads and sequins sown onto the girls' clothes, billowing in plumes of blues, oranges, and greens, the same colors in which women seem to languidly float beneath their burkas as they drift silently by rocky roadside graves.

Past the farmlands toward Peshawar, mountains rise from dried streambeds chalked with salt, which bleaches the scent of the fields as the road climbs into dark folds of flinty gray banded with swaths of rust and black. Skeletal trees and spindly weeds give way to thin grasses of yellow and green that leave the crooked peaks looking as though they were blown with colored dust.

After several hours on the road, Hayat and Lindh arrived once again in Peshawar, where Hayat settled Lindh into his uncle's house in the Civil Quarters area.

"In Peshawar he was going here and there, to the Internet

club and other places," said Hayat, who pointed Lindh to an Internet café and a mosque near his uncle's house when they arrived. Hayat claims he left Lindh alone shortly after the two arrived at his uncle's house, heading out to run errands while Lindh roamed the city on his own. Then, Hayat insists, he didn't see Lindh for about forty-eight hours, until he ran into him by chance at a Civil Quarters mosque called Almadina, where many area residents go for daily prayers. Hayat said he remembers Lindh being with a group of men whom Hayat didn't recognize. The two said hello, and then Lindh told Hayat that he was leaving Peshawar on his own.

"He said I want to go from here," Hayat recalled. "So he went and he didn't tell me where he was going. If he had told me where he was going and with whom, I might have stopped him. But he didn't tell me anything."

It was the last time, Hayat said, that he saw Lindh. "What could I do?" he asked. "I don't know where he went."

At the house of Hayat's uncle, Lindh had left behind a sleeping bag and a few other belongings, winnowing his possessions further still. Hayat returned to Bannu angry with Lindh.

"I showed him all of Pakistan," Hayat said. "When he left us, I left him."

Iltimas was also upset about Lindh's disappearance, especially after hearing from Lindh's mother. Shortly after Lindh left, a letter from Marilyn Walker arrived at Iltimas's madrassa. Postmarked July 2, 2001, the envelope was addressed to "Suleyman Lindh/Suleyman al-Faris" care of Iltimas. Since Lindh was gone, Iltimas opened the note, which his mother began with "Dear Suleyman"; she went on to beg him to call home anytime of day until he reached her.

Tuesdays and Thursdays after 2 PM (Pacific Standard Time) and weekends are best. Or, write and give me a way to reach you. I'll be leaving for the Sundance July 28 and should be back August 13. I hope that we hear from you before then. . . . I really need to hear your voice, John! So, please call "collect" and tell me what's up.

Iltimas put the letter aside, thinking he would save it for Lindh whenever he returned. Nine days later another letter from Marilyn Walker arrived, this one addressed to Iltimas himself. Lindh's mother told Iltimas that she had lost touch with her son, "Suleyman Lindh (Suleyman al-Faris)":

The last I heard from him (via e-mail) was April 26th. He said that he might be moving into the mountains for a cooler climate during the summer months. Would you know where he is and how I may reach him or could you get a message to him to call home "collect" or write?

Lindh's mother included her address and phone number in the note, as well as a copy of the letter in Urdu. Iltimas saw Hayat in the Bannu bazaar shortly thereafter and told him about the letters.

"Where have you been and where's my former pupil?" Iltimas said to Hayat. "His mother is looking for him and asking me about him."

Hayat told Iltimas that he had heard in the bazaar that Lindh had indeed made it north. A customer at Hayat's store, who had recently been in Mansehra, due north of Islamabad, had seen Lindh. Hayat swore he could not remember who told him about Lindh and that he knew nothing else about where he was or what he was doing.

Iltimas relayed this in a lengthy reply to Marilyn Walker dated July 27, 2001. Iltimas told Lindh's mother how he got her letter a "few days back but unfortunately due to various reasons I could not reply in time. Sorry for the delay." He continued:

John Lindh/Suleyman Faris is no doubt your son, but rest assured that he is my student and also my younger brother. He is a very sweet, honest, God-fearing and a very decent human being. All of us who know him, give you credit for being the mother of a person like Suleyman Faris. May Allah give him a happy and a prosperous life "amen."

Suleyman came to me on 30th November 2000, and left on 15th May 2001. He stayed with me for about five and a half months, and during this period he stayed as a student guest. We all looked after him as a member of our family. All my friends, relatives have re-spected and given him the highest regards, all because of his own decency, and everyone has been impressed with his character.

Khizar Hayat is the person who met Suleyman in America. He was there with a missionary team (Tablighi Jamaat). When Khizar Hayat came back to Pakistan, Suleyman left for Yemen. They kept in contact by writing to each other. It was probably October 2000 that Suleyman came to Pakistan on a "visit visa." Mr. Khizar Hayat met him at Islamabad airport, from where he took him to various cities and gave him a round of the religious schools and institutions. He was also shown my small village institute/madrassa. Suleyman decided to stay with me and I was happy to welcome him.

During the summer season, the weather became very hot in Bannu. Suleyman requested that during this period he would like to go to some cooler place. I spoke to Mr. Khizar Hayat regarding Suleyman's wish and handed him over on 15 May 2001. After a couple of weeks I asked Mr. Khizar Hayat about the whereabouts of Suleyman, and I was told that he had gone up into the hills ahead of Mansehra to Batrasi. This area is ahead of the northern town of Abbottabad.

Since his departure, Suleyman has not made any contact with me. Your letter addressed to him is with me, and rest assured, Madam, whenever he contacts me, I will definitely convey your feel-ings to him.

I will also, in my own way, start inquiries to know about his location and health. He is like a younger brother to me and I will spare no efforts to know about his welfare.

May All Mighty Allah shower his blessings on you and your family (Amen).

Lindh's mother still had heard nothing from her son when she wrote Iltimas once more. In a letter dated August 19, 2001, she thanked Iltimas deeply.

I cannot tell you how much it means to me to know that he is cared for by so many in a land so far from home. I appreciate your concern for his well-being and your offer to seek information about his whereabouts. We miss him very much. It isn't like him to have gone so long without making contact with us. If you are able to make contact with Suleyman and he is able to phone home, please tell him to do so "collect."

She signed off by giving her phone numbers and telling Iltimas to call her "any time with any news you may have about him."

Iltimas, in fact, made little effort to find Lindh despite panicked pleas from the boy's mother and his promise to spare no effort in searching for his wayward pupil. Iltimas asked people at Bannu madrassas and mosques who had recently traveled in Pakistan if they had seen Lindh, but no one had. He made plans to go to Mansehra himself, but put them off initially to attend a month-long religious conference near Lahore and then canceled them altogether after September 11.

"I tried to search for him, asking around at madrassas," he said of his initial efforts in Bannu. "After that [September 11] it was impossible for me to search for him, though I tried."

On the whole, Iltimas felt the matter rested with Hayat anyway. "I handed him over to Khizar Hayat," Iltimas said. "He brought him, and he took him."

The summer wore on in Bannu, and Iltimas heard nothing more from Lindh's mother or Lindh, until the news of his capture made world headlines. Neither Iltimas nor Hayat seemed surprised to learn that their onetime Islamic pupil had enlisted first with Harkat ul Mujaheddin and then the Taliban. Both Iltimas and Hayat seemed disappointed in Lindh, rather than angry with him for abandoning his studies to take up arms, a calling both men saw as just.

Hayat and Iltimas maintained through and through that they had no ties to the Taliban or Harkat ul Mujaheddin and did nothing to encourage Lindh's turn toward militancy, which they claimed he hid from them.

"I wanted him to learn Islam, obey all the commands of the religion and then teach the American people exactly what Islam is," Hayat said.

I asked Hayat whether Lindh's choice to join the Taliban went against what he and Iltimas had instilled in him as an aspiring Muslim scholar. He shrugged. "It would have been better if he had gotten his education here in Pakistan and gone back to America and worked there for Islam," Hayat said. "That's what he should have done."

Overall, Hayat painted the picture of his relationship with Lindh as one of an Islamic missionary guiding a hopeful Muslim convert toward a similar path of peaceful proselytizing in the United States. To Hayat, Lindh was a lost missionary, though gone to a worthy alternative cause.

At the time, Hayat's story seemed plausible, and he struck me as sincere, if laconic and temperamental, except in one regard. He claimed to have no idea who, if not he and Iltimas, might have introduced Lindh to members of Harkat ul Mujaheddin. Hayat said Lindh met many people in Bannu, people Hayat didn't know.

"He was meeting so many people, who knows who he was

talking to?" Hayat said, speaking to me one afternoon as I sat with him at his father's store in the bazaar, taking the same seat where Lindh would often studiously read his Koran.

Hayat's complete unwillingness to name anyone among the people he saw Lindh talking with in the bazaar and at the Bannu mosques left me thinking that he either helped arrange Lindh's initial enlistment with Harkat ul Mujaheddin or knew exactly who did. But Hayat remained unwavering in his account whenever I confronted him with doubts and said that I should take up any unanswered questions with the one person who knew all, Lindh himself.

"He's alive, you can ask him," Hayat said, confident, no doubt, that Lindh would not name him, at least not to someone like me.

Iltimas often said the same thing when I voiced doubts about the validity of his recollections and pressed him on whether he knew more than he was telling about Lindh's thoughts and actions during his time at the madrassa.

Iltimas bristled at the suggestion that he knew, or even suspected, that Lindh's wish to go north was tied to the widely known presence of jihadi training camps in the area. Like Hayat, Iltimas washed his hands completely of having anything to do with helping Lindh go on jihad. But he stopped well short of condemning Lindh for doing it. For Iltimas and Hayat, Lindh's two closest friends in Pakistan, there was no question. The Taliban and their Muslim brethren waging struggles in Pakistan and India were righteous before God, and their missions were at least as worthy as any other Islamic undertaking, if not more so.

Indeed, Iltimas and Hayat saw Lindh's ultimate choice to join the Taliban as perhaps not the best decision, but still a good one, however much they denied being involved in it. If taken as truth, the stories Iltimas and Hayat tell implicate them as, at the very least, complicit in Lindh's journey toward Afghanistan. At worst, they encouraged, or even arranged, his crossing from student to jihadi, although both fiercely deny doing either.

In the end, however, Lindh clearly held the choice in his own hands. Hayat may have brought Lindh to Iltimas and taken him away—but only at Lindh's bidding. Lindh came and went as he chose and appeared to allow Iltimas, Hayat, and others to play roles in his life as characters he understood, perhaps even used.

"Shakespeare said, 'Oh, frailty, thy name is woman,'" Iltimas quoted one afternoon in an attempt to create an analogy. His groping, garbled allusion to the Bard in his heavily accented English came off sounding appropriately bizarre. The two of us were standing on the roof of his madrassa, where we had a view of the village houses around the school. I tried not to laugh as he went on, sweeping an arm toward the horizon for dramatic effect. "I said to Suleyman, 'Oh, Suleyman, thy life is history.'"

☪

Standing unassumingly behind red brick walls near a dusty playground, the Almadina mosque where Hayat said he last saw Lindh draws a varied crowd. Most of the followers are government workers who live in the surrounding Civil Quarters. Tablighi Jamaat missionaries favor the mosque as well. So do members of Harkat ul Mujaheddin, who gather at Almadina largely because of Imam Hizbullah, a prayer leader with close ties to the militant group.

Heavily backed by the Pakistani military, Harkat ul Mujaheddin emerged as a force in the Kashmir insurgency in 1994 and quickly grew into one of the largest and most feared of Pakistan's many militant organizations. By 1997, the group had earned a ranking on the State Department's list of foreign terrorist organizations and taken on an especially dark reputation for its alleged involvement in several bloody kidnappings, most of which they denied. In 1995, the group reportedly abducted six foreign tourists trekking in Kashmir. One captive, American John Childs, escaped, but the rest of the group remained in the hands of the militants, who aired ransom demands to New Delhi that were refused. A month after the trekkers first disappeared, the corpse of Norwegian hiker Hans Christian Ostro was found, decapitated, head in lap. The kidnapping, ransom demands, and killing style were to form a grisly signature that appeared again in the murder of *Wall Street Journal* correspondent Daniel Pearl in the early weeks of 2002. Harkat ul Mujaheddin was again believed to have been involved, along with another militant group named Jaish-e-Mohammed, or Army of Mohammed, in the reporter's death. Abducted in Karachi, Pearl suffered the same fate as Ostro, only Pearl's murder was captured on videotape later handed to U.S. authorities.

The Pakistani government stepped up its halting efforts against Harkat ul Mujaheddin and other groups banned in the wake of September 11 after Pearl's murder. But during the years of the Taliban's rule in Afghanistan, Pakistani authorities worked closely with both Harkat ul Mujaheddin and the Taliban to run an underground jihadi railroad of sorts that stretched from Kandahar, Afghanistan, to Shrinagar, Kashmir. Throughout the 1990s, Harkat ul Mujaheddin and like-minded militants traveled a network of madrassas and training camps that stretched through India, Pakistan, and Afghanistan, where the group's work with the Taliban at times overlapped with the terrorist activities of Osama bin Laden, then living in Afghanistan under Taliban protection.

The whole thing was a family affair for Almadina mosque prayer leader Imam Hizbullah, whose father Ubaid Ullah had been a provincial religious leader who had counted longtime Harkat ul Mujaheddin leadership figures among his closest friends. "We had the same ideology," Hizbullah said. "All of us are Muslims with the same mission."

Hizbullah had once undergone Harkat ul Mujaheddin training to brush up on the fighting skills he initially learned in Afghanistan, where he spent a summer break from madrassa studies as a frontline relief fighter in 1996, a common summer break activity for madrassa students in Pakistan. But jihad was to take a back seat with Hizbullah after Ubaid Ullah died in Chitral during sectarian clashes in 1999. Hizbullah then assumed the head role at his father's Peshawar madrassa and began preaching at Almadina close by, taking on many of his late father's political practices, as well as his religious duties. Hizbullah kept up family ties with Harkat ul Mujaheddin and used both the mosque and the madrassa as harbors for Taliban volunteers and Kashmir jihadis. During his work as a religious leader, Hizbullah also helped scores of eager volunteer jihadis enlist to fight with the Taliban and Harkut ul Mujaheddin.

"In 1998, 1999, when my father was alive, Arabs used to come to this mosque," said Hizbullah, a thin man in his late twenties. "When my father was alive he handled these problems. After he died people began coming to me."

Sitting on the floor in a dark, cramped sideroom thick with flies at Almadina, Hizbullah talked into his lap, letting his shaggy black hair hang over his ruddy face as he described how before September 11 he served as an unofficial recruiter for jihadi groups. In this position, he assisted young Islamic militants from overseas looking to fight in either Kashmir or Afghanistan.

Hizbullah did not recognize Lindh from a picture shown to him and did not recall ever seeing him at the madrassa. That meant little, since Hizbullah had long ago lost count of how many foreigners from places like Chechnya, Sudan, Egypt, Syria, and other countries he helped cross into Afghanistan and Kashmir. He said "hundreds" of volunteers had drifted through Almadina's doors, where, as of early 2002, photocopied articles from local newspapers and magazines voicing support for the Taliban, Mullah Mohammed Omar, and Osama bin Laden hung.

Most volunteers needed little help from Hizbullah before September 11, as Harkat ul Mujaheddin and other groups were carrying on legally with recruiting and propaganda offices open in Peshawar and other cities around Pakistan.

"Before September 11, when the situation was normal, people used to go directly to the Harkat office," Hizbullah said, adding that Lindh, if he had ever even been there, likely met someone among the Almadina congregation from Harkat ul Mujaheddin and signed on like so many other foreigners with little ado. "Harkat ul Mujaheddin is not like an army or any other force," Hizbullah said. "They're common people. Everyone is Harkat ul Mujaheddin. . . . If they're coming here and praying, you cannot say who is Harkat and who is a common man."

I asked Hizbullah if he could point me to someone among the Harkat ul Mujaheddin ranks in Peshawar who might be able to tell me specifically who had brought Lindh to their recruitment office. He advised me not to introduce myself to any Harkat ul Mujaheddin members since I was an American, but he offered to ask his Harkat ul Mujaheddin contacts himself and get back to me with anything he found out. I gave him a picture of Lindh, which he took around to Harkat ul Mujaheddin members in Peshawar over the course of several days. He found answers easily. The young American was well remembered. Hizbullah's friends in Harkat ul Mujaheddin told him that Lindh had been brought to them by a Tablighi Jamaat member from Bannu named Khizar Hayat.

Upon his capture, Lindh told U.S. investigators that an acquaintance escorted him to the Harkat ul Mujaheddin office in Peshawar. There, recruiters interviewed him over the course of a few days before sending him to a paramilitary camp near a northern mountain town called Mansehra.

Hizbullah shed a little more light on what sounded like the laid-back recruitment process of the militant group. "In Harkat ul Mujaheddin there's no regular membership," he said. "Anyone who wants to get training can go to Harkat. If anyone comes to us, to Harkat, wanting training to go for jihad, we send them to Mansehra for basic training. Once he gets the training, he's a member. If he doesn't want to work with Harkat, he can go. If he wants to come back and join at a later time, he's allowed."

☪

Mansehra seems an odd place for a militant stronghold. Compared to Bannu or even Peshawar, it appears comfortably ordinary, with sturdy block buildings lining relatively tidy streets curving through the hills at the foot of Kashmir's upper reaches in the Himalayas. Satellite dishes and antennae for televisions and mobile phones clutter rooftops, rising in spidery tendrils alongside tall minarets that line a horizon ringed by distant snowcaps shrouded in heavy clouds. On the streets, cars and trucks move slowly through foot traffic in the twisting lanes, which house a colorful bazaar full of modern wares, like shiny pots and pans, polished leathers, and handsomely tailored clothes. Far fewer beards and beggars fill the crowds, where women wearing scarves over their heads walk easily alongside the men, moving busily under the colored waves of rugs, scarves, and shawls hanging in the breeze over storefronts.

Past the bazaar, a cluster of large walled houses crowd a quiet hilltop in the center of town, where Harkat ul Mujaheddin once rented a nondescript two-story brick villa to serve as its area administrative headquarters and guesthouse. Harkat ul Mujaheddin volunteer fighters from all over Pakistan would journey to Mansehra and check in at the house before being shown to the actual training camp, which sat high in a chain of wooded hills shouldering the city.

Before September 11, Harkat ul Mujaheddin and other militant organizations ran camps at Mansehra and other locations across Pakistan and Afghanistan with the approval, and even assistance, of the Pakistani military and the country's spy agency, the Interservices Intelligence (ISI). However, by April 2002, Pakistani authorities had shuttered Harkat ul Mujaheddin's Mansehra office and demolished the nearby camp.

A wave of arrests in Mansehra and elsewhere in Pakistan led to the jailing of dozens of Harkat ul Mujaheddin political leaders, trainers, and fighters, along with hundreds of their counterparts from Pakistan's other newly banned militant groups. In a span of months, Harkat ul Mujaheddin and other militant organizations, longtime loyal purveyors of Islamabad's policy toward Kashmir and Afghanistan, had become pariahs due to Pakistani ruler Pervez Musharraf's abrupt political realignment after September 11.

Local police raided Harkat ul Mujaheddin's Mansehra residence in late March 2002, capturing some twenty fighters on hand and emptying the shelves and cabinets that filled the rooms of nearly all books, files, and weapons. A few scattered belongings, mostly readings about Kashmir and Islam, remained when the landowner opened the doors again to let carpenters begin renovations in the hope of sprucing the place up for new renters.

A few Harkat ul Mujaheddin members themselves had also been left behind in Mansehra, having gone into hiding after evading arrest. Some of them quietly ventured to the house on occasion once it was opened again, looking for any items to salvage there and from their nearby rented storage shed. Among those who slipped into the house in the spring of 2002 was Talha, a twenty-one-year-old Harkat ul Mujaheddin fighter who trained with Lindh in the summer of 2001.

When Lindh arrived in Mansehra, about one hundred young Harkat ul Mujaheddin volunteers like Talha were already at the training camp above town, undergoing physical conditioning, combat lessons, and religious instruction. Lindh had traveled to Mansehra alone after being told where to go and whom to contact by his Harkat ul Mujaheddin recruiters in Peshawar. Talha, whose name is an alias, remembered Lindh's arrival well since he was the only foreigner in training at the time.

"Our instructor introduced him on his third day at lunch," Talha recalled from the training days when he first met Lindh, whom recruits in Mansehra knew as Abdul Hamid. "One of our colleagues who understands English told us what Abdul Hamid was saying," said Talha, whose splotchy beard seemed to be falling out, rather than growing in, framing an underbite full of ragged, dirty teeth. "He asked those of us who knew Islam and its history to sit with him so he could learn more. He said that when he talked about Islam it gave him a new life."

Originally from Karachi, Talha appeared an unlikely trained killer from one of the most violent jihadi groups, as he thumbed grungy pink prayer beads with long, delicate fingers. His fine hands matched his tall, lanky frame, which seemed folded into his oversized aqua shalwar qamiz. Talha's boyish face held an edge nonetheless that he accentuated with the traditional kohl eyeliner fashionable among Islamic militants in Pakistan and Afghanistan. Smiling as he remembered their first days together, Talha showed no trace of fierceness when he talked of Lindh. Neither did others who had trained in the camp during those days.

"When he was here in the camp he studied the Koran," said Abdullah, a chunky fighter with a wedge-shaped bushy beard hanging from a flat face stretched beneath a folded brow. Abdullah also used an alias when talking with me at the Harkat ul Mujaheddin house in Mansehra. And like Talha, he beamed when he spoke of Lindh, who had become a sort of teen idol in Pakistan's jihadi ranks.

"He said he studied mostly about jihad," Abdullah said. "He said he came to the Mansehra camp to see the jihadi environment and that he hadn't seen such an environment anywhere."

Lindh's instructors afforded him no special status, despite his unique background. "He was a common man in the camp like us," Talha said. "He was equal."

Lindh slept on a threadbare bed in a tent like all the other recruits, underwent the same daily schedule of drills, classes, and prayers, and ate the same humble camp meals. But, as he had been in Bannu, he was a curiosity, the subject of close observation, gossip, and even a touch of reverence. "When we were sitting at lunch or dinner, we would all try to sit next to him," Talha said.

Lindh's inability to speak any of the local languages left him heavily dependent on his chief instructor, a Harkat ul Mujaheddin fighter from Indian Kashmir who spoke English and often translated for Lindh when he spoke in the group sessions.

"His instructor's name was Farooq," offered Hamid, one of roughly ten Harkat ul Mujaheddin trainers who were at the camp during Lindh's time. "He was from Indian-held Kashmir. He embraced martyrdom there."

Also going by an alias, Hamid said Farooq died in clashes with the Indian army across Pakistan's eastern border in early October 2001.

Aged twenty-seven, Hamid was short, with stubby hands and a dark, doughy face beneath his smoothed beard. He wore tiny square glasses with a smoky tint that matched his neatly pressed charcoal shalwar qamiz. Probably owing to his superior position of trainer, he carried an unmistakable air of authority among the other Harkat ul Mujaheddin fighters left in Mansehra. Hamid spoke thoughtfully, at length, with surprising candor about the goings on in the camp and Lindh's days there. Hamid did not get to know Lindh all that well, since his time at the camp was short and the nature of the routine kept socializing to a mostly superficial level. "Our main concern in the camp is ensuring that the volunteers take the cause seriously," Hamid said. "We didn't waste our time forming friendships. We focused on the training."

Hamid and others got to know Lindh perhaps a bit more deeply nonetheless since he drew a level of attention above the average Pakistani recruits. Hamid would often speak with Lindh during daily breaks and sometimes pulled him aside for a few moments between classes to chat in a friendly way.

"He was an ideological Muslim. What I saw in Suleyman, he was honest and trustworthy. He stood apart because he converted to Islam, whereas the rest of us were born Muslims," Hamid said. "Suleyman was the best Muslim because he embraced Islam after studying the religion and thinking deeply about it. Such Muslims are more sincere. I was not his instructor, but as a fellow teacher I watched his progress. He spent a month here. We keep a record of everyone who comes here, but since the government demolished our camp that record is lost. When Suleyman was here, there were many volunteers. Due to his language problem, he was withdrawn. He was a quiet one. He sought to emulate the prophet. He always used to thumb his prayer beads, saying the name of God over and over again."

Hamid remembered Lindh as studious, recalling how he often saw him reading during his free time at the camp. Lindh's free time for reading was limited, though, since an average day of training was demanding.

During the twenty-four-day course, recruits awoke before dawn and gathered at the camp mosque, where they opened Korans and recited verses until the first azzan sounded. After morning prayer, the instructors put recruits through two hours of physical training that involved running and calisthenics. Then came breakfast, which the group ate quickly before arms lessons, in which the instructors schooled the trainees in the use of pistols, Kalashnikovs, explosives, and combat tactics.

The sparse camp consisted of little more than a guesthouse, mosque, office, and building to house the arms used in training.

"We taught assembling and breaking down weapons," Hamid said. "We also taught weapons techniques. In the same class we taught how to handle weapons and how to fire, as well as guerrilla warfare skills. We only train in small arms. We also taught night fighting skills and ambush strategy."

The recruits were given free time in the afternoon when arms lessons were done. In the evening, the trainees gathered again in the mosque for an informal group meeting before dinner, which ended shortly before the call to evening prayer.

After the fifth and final prayer of the day the students grouped for what they called an "accountability session," in which the instructors encouraged trainees to air any grievances they had with classmates in order to openly resolve issues or conflicts that arose in the ranks.

"We didn't allow anyone in the camp to abuse or have a quarrel with someone else," Hamid said. "If someone has a complaint about another volunteer, he stands up and voices it in front of the group. Suleyman never complained about anyone, and no one complained about Suleyman."

The regimen of conditioning and indoctrination provided basic training to prepare, in the shortest possible time, volunteer fighters for Kashmir and Afghanistan, where steady death tolls ensured a constant need for fresh recruits.

Most of the volunteers in Lindh's training class never actually fought; they went home instead. A select few from each class would normally be chosen to undergo advanced guerrilla instruction at another Harkat ul Mujaheddin camp. After the most promising recruits finished advanced guerrilla training, the ISI organized them into small bands and sent them on guerrilla missions in Kashmir, roughly ten miles from the Mansehra facility. Fighters not chosen for Kashmir may have the option of going to Afghanistan, where Harkat ul Mujaheddin also worked to aid the Taliban in its long-running war against the Northern Alliance.

"We train volunteers in the most basic skills they need in Afghanistan," Hamid said. "One doesn't need advanced guerrilla training to go to Afghanistan because the war there is not so difficult. The enemy is in front of you and you're shooting at him. But war in Kashmir is the most difficult. You need advanced training to fight there. You face the enemy on all sides in Kashmir."

Lindh threw himself wholly into the training regimen, impressing his instructors and fellow trainees alike with his ardor for becoming a skilled fighter. "He was no laggard," Hamid said.

Though Lindh demonstrated an unflinching devotion to jihad through his eagerness in training, Lindh's skills as a fighter fell short in the eyes of his instructors. As a result, the instructors passed over Lindh when choosing recruits for intensive guerrilla training at one of Harkat ul Mujaheddin's other camps in Pakistani Kashmir.

"We have a procedure for advanced guerrilla training," Hamid said. "We select the best volunteers for that. We send only handpicked volunteers for that training, and Suleyman didn't qualify. We chose the stronger volunteers. Most of them are from hilly areas. Suleyman was from an American city. He was soft. We pick volunteers with a lot of strength and endurance. Suleyman was not fit enough, although he was sincere."

After the impression of Harkat ul Mujaheddin Lindh had gotten in the camp, he apparently felt okay about being overlooked for special grooming as a Kashmir insurgent. Over the month of training, he had learned that in reality the Harkat ul Mujaheddin might not live up to their image as the jihadi heroes put forth in local propagandas. He had thought Harkat ul Mujaheddin was mounting a grassroots struggle to free Kashmir from the brutal hold of Indian oppression, but clearly the Pakistani government was using the jihadis as cheap labor for its geopolitical aims.

Pakistan's militants, government officials, and religious leaders base their public support for Kashmir on an argument of democracy for the region. In reality, though, none of the Pakistanis who have helped the Kashmiris wage their struggle really believes that Kashmir, a landlocked area, could ever be anything but a state within Pakistan. While some may claim Kashmir should accede to Pakistan for the sake of Islamic brotherhood, Pakistan wants the area for strategic reasons as well.

One day Lindh had seen a Pakistani map in the camp that dramatically changed his thinking about the Kashmir conflict. The map showed the disputed border region where he and others were supposed to have fought. On the map, Kashmir appeared as a part of Pakistan, not demarcated as an independent state. Lindh had gone into the camp thinking he and the other Harkat ul Mujaheddin volunteers were aiding the Muslims of Kashmir in a bid for independence from India, not in accession to Pakistan.

Lindh was waking up to the foul politics Pakistan plays with the Kashmir conflict. The mujaheddin trained in the camps around Mansehra and elsewhere weren't freedom fighters at all. Seeing how the ISI worked in the Harkat ul Mujaheddin camp made it clear that the Pakistani government was preying on the young men's idealistic intentions and sending them to fight inside India as irregulars, where uniformed soldiers could not go without risking full reprisal by the Indian army. In sending volunteer jihadis into Kashmir, Pakistan was able to maintain plausible deniability, thereby avoiding a direct military confrontation with India, which had already trounced Pakistan three times in war.

Members of the ISI feared that any foreigners, particularly Westerners, allowed to see the workings of the camps might later disclose the government's direct involvement in the Kashmir insurgency, a revelation that could invite another disastrous war with India. But the jihadis in groups like Harkat ul Mujaheddin went by a code rooted in religion, not Pakistani policy, and so they welcomed foreign volunteers like Lindh, despite objections from ISI. The presence of ISI officers in the camp had surprised Lindh. Whenever they showed up, he was told to hide, although he was never told why. Lindh had seen Kashmir as a brave cause when he was sitting in Bannu absorbing government and jihadi propaganda. At the camp, he began to understand the conflict for what it was, an effort by Pakistan to bleed its neighbor and nuclear rival, India, by keeping up guerrilla attacks on military and civilian targets.

Lindh wanted out. He kept the ill feelings he began to have about Kashmir to himself, but told his Harkat ul Mujaheddin trainers toward the end of his stay in the camp that he wanted to do his jihad in Afghanistan, not Kashmir. He still felt committed to the idea that he had to perform some sort of jihad, just not in Kashmir. In addition to becoming disenchanted with the cause, Lindh was also growing more attached to the Taliban after hearing more about Afghanistan from people in the camp. Lindh's Harkat ul Mujaheddin trainers saw no problem sending him off to Afghanistan, naturally, since they thought he would be useless in Kashmir anyway. But Talha and other Harkat volunteers Lindh befriended urged the boy to stay with them before he left.

"We didn't want him to go to Afghanistan," Talha said. But

Lindh told them he needed to see the Islam of Afghanistan for himself and that he felt he should go right away. "He said he was sure he would be punished when he returned to America, so he wanted to see Afghanistan first," Talha said. "He planned to see Islamic society for himself, to see the true Islam."

Like Iltimas, Hamid and the other Harkat ul Mujaheddin leaders in the Mansehra area didn't question Lindh's reasons. They simply shuffled him on to Afghanistan, where he was to become a fighter of the lowest rank in one of the world's most obscure wars, just as thousands of other jihadis had done before him with help from militant groups like Harkat ul Mujaheddin.

"I don't know why Suleyman chose to go to Afghanistan, but I think he was animated by seeing cruelty against Muslims all over the world," Hamid said. "The other reason he went was to see the Islamic government of the Taliban and the Taliban lifestyle. I think he didn't go to fight, because all of our volunteers go to Kashmir if they want to fight."

There were a few wrinkles, though, given Lindh's unique background as an American. "Suleyman's case was a little bit different," Hamid said, describing how Lindh's inability to speak with locals prevented him from going directly from Mansehra to Afghanistan. "We could not send him with anyone, so we sent him to our Peshawar office and they arranged his trip to Afghanistan."

Lindh returned to Harkat ul Mujaheddin's Peshawar office and told them he had changed his mind about jihad in Kashmir and wanted to fight in Afghanistan instead. As in Mansehra, no one objected or raised questions. Jihad was jihad, whether in Afghanistan or in Kashmir, as far as the Harkat ul Mujaheddin recruiters at the Peshawar office were concerned. They wrote Lindh a letter of recommendation and told him where to go and whom to see in Kabul. They hooked him up with a ride, but didn't go with him. Instead, they introduced Lindh to two Pakistani businessmen who were also on their way into Afghanistan, and the three shared a hired car to the border. Before Lindh left Peshawar, however, he wrote a note to his mom and asked the Peshawar recruiters to mail it for him. He told her that he was travelling into Afghanistan to perform "humanitarian work." She never received the letter.

CHAPTER FIVE

The Taliban Caravan

THE main road from Peshawar to Afghanistan rises through the Kyber Pass, corkscrewing through vacant desert canyons that unfold a corner of the Safed Range at a border crossing called Torkam. Toting aging Kalashnikovs, mustached Pakistani border guards wearing dusty navy uniforms and tattered berets man a checkpoint at the gates—two huge, blue metal doors, rusted and wind battered, hung on a gap in the mountainside. On any given day the crossing is a chaotic scene, with the weary Pakistani authorities hopelessly trying to police a backup of overloaded trucks and huge crowds pressing against both sides of the gates. Drivers for hire wearing turbans and shawls idle rattletrap taxis along the road on either side of the border, turning the stretch into a long parking lot threaded by a ribbon of blacktop roamed by peddlers selling soft drinks, snacks, or whatever they can. Children with wheelbarrows dart through the crowds and back and forth across the border freely, carting luggage for the many travelers who drive to the crossing in one car, walk through the gates, and then pick up another ride because Pakistani authorities allow few vehicles to move freely through the pass.

Getting from Pakistan to Afghanistan in a car through the Torkam gates can be difficult, but slipping across the border on foot is easy. Lindh was without the Pakistani travel permits one normally needs to present at the dilapidated immigration office next to the gates on the Pakistani side of the border. He might have been able to drift through the checkpoint even so, letting himself fall into the stream of unchecked travelers moving on foot through the crossing. But he didn't want to risk being stopped and potentially turned back on the off chance that the Pakistani guards would be exercising their spotty border enforcement as he passed. Lindh's Pakistani traveling companions knew another way, the route traveled by uncounted thousands of Afghan refugees. Lindh and the two Pakistani businessmen had the hired car from Peshawar drop them off well short of the scene at the Torkam gates. Then they hiked into the surrounding hills, edging along footpaths worn by the droves who had fled Afghanistan over the years, until they emerged on the other side of the frontier near the gates. There they quickly found another taxi, which drove them from the border to Jalalabad and on to Kabul.

For some distance, the pot-holed road runs along the Kabul River, streaming gray and flat through marshes that floor a valley of barren, flinty reaches outside Jalalabad. Mountains rise higher as the river narrows farther west, cutting through fissured valley walls mottled with the color of blackened rust. An hour or so outside Kabul, the road climbs in gut-twisting turns through canyons, where drivers must weave through the wreckage of the scattered and destroyed Soviet tanks and armored personnel carriers. Heading up to the plains west of Kabul, sandy slopes pool around rocky tendrils fingering the flats just before the city, spread in ruins, appears through a blue haze of pollution and dust.

Arriving in Kabul, Lindh was shown to a heavily guarded compound near the city center where Taliban recruiters were to size him up for possible enlistment. The five concrete slab buildings, painted yellow, served as an enlistment office and guesthouse for foreign Taliban volunteers, whom locals watched come and go from a distance. If anything might have given Lindh pause as he spent his first hours in Afghanistan, it would have been the view from the windows of those compound offices. Outside, two gutted palaces known as Dar ul-Anan stand on twin hilltops, their gaping facades seemingly a colorless reflection of the flat miles of shattered neighborhoods spread below them. Whole tracts of the city had been destroyed in the brutal struggles for control of Kabul during the 1990s. The ruined districts surrounding the palace buildings and the office Lindh visited form a labyrinth of blasted houses and fallen walls. The area looks as though a massive earthquake has leveled the neighborhoods, somehow leaving only the compound, built in recent years, intact.

Inside, that first day, several Taliban fighters, some of whom would later fight alongside him, questioned Lindh over the course of many interviews. He told them he was an American and that he wanted to go to the front lines to fight against the Northern Alliance. His Taliban recruiters were unimpressed by his time with Harkat ul Mujaheddin. They determined that he needed more combat expertise in order to fight in Afghanistan, experience they were willing to give him through further training.

Lindh objected, telling the recruiters that he wanted to go to the front right away. Harkat ul Mujaheddin had told him in Peshawar that he had enough training to go straight to the front lines with the Taliban, and he thought the letter of introduction he carried, which he couldn't read because it was either written in Pashto or Urdu, was his ticket. The recruiters told him he didn't have a choice in the matter. If you want to go on jihad for the Taliban, they told him, you must get more training. Lindh relented and his recruiters began to make arrangements for his training.

Again, Lindh's inability to speak local languages posed a problem. One might find an English-speaking militant trainer in

Pakistan, since the language remained widely spoken as a legacy of British colonialism. Not so in Afghanistan.

Lindh's fluency in Arabic, however, meant he could train at camps set up especially for Arabic-speaking volunteers, where the curriculum included training in basic battlefield skills like heavy weapons and guerrilla techniques, as well as terrorist practices like bomb making and assassinations. There he was to receive two more weeks of combat training before heading to the front, fighting with the Taliban as part of a brigade of foreign jihadis called Ansar, or helpers. Osama bin Laden funded the Arab camps, but Lindh's Taliban recruiters made no mention of bin Laden or al-Qaida. They simply told Lindh he should go to an address in Kandahar, where someone would show him to an Arab training camp. Lindh was soon traveling south.

Midsummer had settled over the low desert between Kabul and Kandahar, a span of sandy plains running beside a dried-up river known as the Tarnak Rud, which sits between two long ranges of spiny mountains trailing down from the upper Hindu Kush. The blacktop road curving down and out from the rocky rises surrounding Kabul gradually cracks up as it trails from the capital into the twenty hours of otherworldly scenes stretched across the wasteland between the two cities. Camels and nomads drift through a desert haze the color of bone kicked up by dust storms that spin down from the mountains. The heat seems to slow the sparse traffic of heavy trucks, station wagon taxis, and motorcycles ridden by turbaned men in billowing shawls. Drivers often stop by the side of road to pray, kneeling in the swirl of burning dust that powders one's face, cracking dried lips.

Just miles outside Kabul the road turns from broken pavement to gravelly tracks, soon dissolving into nothing more than a sandy path. Roadside cemeteries mark the way, where flags made from rags hanging on bent poles wave over unmarked graves, attesting to the sad fate many have suffered under a two-decade plague of war. Traveling that summer day, Lindh passed through villages with names like Surki, Shah Juy, and Jaldak, lonely bands of houses half buried in sand, seemingly empty until someone appears in the doorway to watch travelers pass.

At the entrance of Kandahar, loose goats wobble through heaps of rusted and empty barrels, metal shipping containers, and stacks of tires sitting beside the road. The piles of refuse serve as the city gates to Kandahar, easily the most desolate and wasted place in Afghanistan. Kandahar, in its sprawl, seems more like a squatters' camp settled on a dumpsite than an actual city. On an average summer day, thin crowds move among the pale shadows cast by unmarked storefronts and shoddy plastic umbrellas, making their way through streets that smell like a well-sunned latrine.

Upon arriving in Kandahar, Lindh spent several nights at an Arab guesthouse, where recruits like Lindh stayed before moving on to one of the two large al-Qaida camps in the area at the time. Lindh reported to al-Farooq for training in June with about twenty other volunteers, mostly from Saudi Arabia.

Al-Farooq, also known to Kandahar locals as Germabak, lies in a forked canyon at the southern end of a rise of mountains named the Shah Maqsud Range, barren ridges that look untouched by water, shaped by the raking wind and heat that sear the surrounding rocky fields. The range is reachable only after a long drive over a confusing web of dirt trails. The switchbacks and unmarked turnoffs run past villages such as Asad and Ziarat-e-Shah Maqsud, no more than a cluster of hovels around wells, a few tilled fields, and more cemeteries, where rows of unmarked headstones stretch for acres before folding seamlessly into the even scatter of blackened stones that blankets the low rolls of the Shah Maqsud floor.

Marked with a simple sign, the camp itself was nestled in

canyons unseen from the plains. The entrance is a horned bluff
where several of the desert tracks slope to a common point at the
head of the twin valleys. In the summer of 2002, al-Farooq sat
empty. Bin Laden's forces abandoned the site shortly after September 11, 2001, fearing American bombs that of course soon
came with the opening attacks by the United States. A troop of
U.S. Marines landed at the site soon thereafter, trashing the camp
in search of clues about al-Qaida. The Marines destroyed what
the bombs hadn't and left behind a calling card drawn huge on a
cliff overlooking the main grounds. "USMC" stands in giant letters spelled out with white painted rocks, previously used as road
markers when the camp was running in full, as it was when Lindh
arrived in early June 2001.

Shortly after his arrival, camp trainers told Lindh that the
course would last six weeks, not two. This information annoyed
and frustrated Lindh again, and the look of the camp did little to
ease his feelings. Al-Farooq was bigger than the Harkat ul Mujaheddin camp, but it offered no comforts. Living in a tent, Lindh
joined about one hundred other Arab volunteers in training at al-
Farooq, where instructors ran a program much like the training
in Mansehra. Instructors woke recruits early and ran them
through a daily regimen of running, hiking, and arms training,
broken up by prayers. The trainees had target practice and
learned how to handle grenades and Molotov cocktails. They
went on camping excursions and learned battlefield tactics such
as different types of combat crawls, surveillance methods, camou-
flage techniques, signs and signals, ways to navigate rugged terrain, and proper methods for carrying weapons.

As in Mansehra, the trainees gathered together in the eve-
·nings at the camp mosque. But instead of accountability sessions,
al-Farooq offered guest speakers every night. Among the lectur-
ers who addressed the group was Osama bin Laden, who showed

up at the camp a handful of times towards the end of Lindh's course.

The evening lectures had always been a chance to nod off for Lindh and other recruits, who sagged at the end of a day's training. Lindh and others struggled to stay awake for all of the speakers, but sitting through a bin Laden lecture required a special kind of endurance. Bin Laden, apparently ill, spoke softly and slowly as he sipped water during his talks, which covered topics ranging from local problems to global politics. Lindh dozed through at least one of bin Laden's lectures and found the others unmemorable, despite bin Laden's obvious stature in the camp.

Lindh had heard rumors that bin Laden masterminded the embassy attacks in East Africa, and he knew that the wealthy Saudi had worked with Azzam and supported jihadi causes. But he had also heard that bin Laden thought that jihadi struggles like Chechnya and Bosnia were lost causes, leaving Lindh uncertain of what to make of him. Also, Lindh disdained the reverence that some in the camp showed bin Laden, who was always accompanied by an unusually large entourage. Lindh felt jihad was not a celebrity cause and that bin Laden's apparent stardom did not mesh with the egalitarian ideals of Islam.

After bin Laden spoke, recruits who wanted to meet him would line up for a handshake. Lindh passed on the first evening, as did some of the other trainees, and went back to his tent to sleep. On one of bin Laden's other visits, however, recruits were told at the end of bin Laden's talk that they could either meet the famed Saudi exile or do camp chores after the mosque session. Some of the camp instructors had told Lindh beforehand that anyone who wanted to meet bin Laden had to be sincere about jihad, since many in the camp seemed ready to drop out. Lindh was indeed serious about jihad and wanted to get out of work detail, so he joined four other trainees, with whom bin Laden spent about five minutes, thanking each for volunteering.

The meeting seemed insignificant to Lindh at the time, an excuse to avoid some unpleasant camp duty. He sat before bin Laden not knowing either that the United States already wanted the terrorist leader for mass murder or that, in those very days, bin Laden was orchestrating the deaths of thousands more. Lindh walked away thinking little of the encounter, eager only to be done with training so he could finally go on duty with the Taliban.

Towards the end of the course, an al-Farooq instructor approached Lindh and others to ask if anyone would be interested in taking up jihad in either Israel or the United States. Lindh and his comrades thought the offer was a trick question, an effort by the Arabs who ran the camp to ferret out spies rumored to be among them. The recruitment was likely for real, however. One of the ranking al-Farooq trainers, Abu Mohammad al-Misri, an Egyptian also known as Shaleh, had been named in a federal indictment for his alleged participation in the 1998 embassy bombings. Again, Lindh knew nothing of him. He turned down the offer to leave Afghanistan, saying for the umpteenth time that he had come to help the Taliban. Lindh's trainers respected his decision and soon granted his wish. Lindh left the camp in June or July at the end of his training. Stomach troubles laid him up for about a week at the Arab house in Kandahar, a lousy start for jihad. When he felt better, Lindh returned to Kabul to join a group of about thirty other Ansar volunteers headed north to fight Northern Alliance forces, which were then clinging to a tiny corner of Afghanistan in a losing war.

☪

Lindh arrived on the front lines in the war's eleventh hour. The fighting between the Taliban and the Northern Alliance had by then worn on for roughly seven years with much of that time spent in stalemate along the front where Lindh wound up serving.

But in the summer of 2001, the conflict seemed to be entering a decisive phase. The Taliban were poised either to rout Ahmed Shah Massoud's forces by breaking up their northern lines or to see them regain important territory that could be used as a springboard for a renewed push south and west over ground hard won by the Taliban.

When Lindh deployed with the Taliban, Massoud's forces held the Panjshir Valley north of Kabul. To hold off the Taliban, they had dynamited the entrance to the Salang Pass, the main route north through the Hindu Kush, so the Taliban sometimes ferried its troops to northern outposts from Kabul to Konduz with airlifts of Antonov cargo planes. This proved easier than traversing a roundabout mountain pass that led to the city of Pole-I-Khomri and onto Konduz and Taloqan, the northernmost frontline towns held by the Taliban.

Lindh's group flew in on one of the last troop lifts from Kabul to Konduz on about September 6, 2001. In Konduz, Lindh was given a Kalashnikov and two grenades, a vest with pockets for his ammunition, and some warmer clothes, since winter was already coming in the mountains. A Taliban commander told Lindh and the others in the group that they were officially members of the Afghan army, even though there was not an Afghan among them. With that, Lindh saw himself as a sworn servant to the Taliban's Islamic Emirate of Afghanistan, a soldier, not a terrorist—a distinction that would come to mean little, if anything, in the eyes of most Americans.

Lindh's unit was then sent toward the front lines in a province called Takhar, where the group was divided into two smaller teams and ordered to take up defensive positions on two hills opposite Northern Alliance forces. Lindh was told his group would make no attacks; their mission was simply to hold the hills — essentially to perform guard duty at a position that weathered only the occasional volley of Northern Alliance mortar fire.

In addition to his gun and grenades, Lindh carried an orange potato sack that held his passport, a few personal belongings, and some books, which he read during the long, boring hours on duty. Lindh's long-anticipated jihad consisted of touring a remote corner of the front line where the Northern Alliance forces were so far away that the Taliban rarely, if ever, saw them. Lindh never managed even to squeeze off a shot across the front lines, and his unit suffered no casualties while protecting the lonely hills. Lindh mostly read and eyed the empty landscape, rotating with others in two-week shifts in and out of foxholes. Since Lindh had heard that the Northern Alliance had a penchant for raping, castrating, and executing captured soldiers, as well as civilians they deemed sympathetic to the Taliban, keeping a safe distance from their positions may have seemed a pretty cushy jihad.

On the other side of the front, the Northern Alliance fighters regarded the foreigners in the trenches opposite them with a mixture of fear, grudging respect, and revulsion. They didn't know that among the foreigners, in addition to some infamously sadistic fighters, were also a number like Lindh, scared one-timers of questionable physical ability and combat expertise. And there were even lesser soldiers among them—a collection of elderly or mentally ill men and misguided youths from a host of Gulf states.

Other Ansar units elsewhere on the front line had more experience and served as the Taliban's vanguard attack force, a group that awed the Alliance with its military prowess and bravery. Many foreign fighters who had committed themselves to Afghanistan's front were fearsome indeed, radicalized by rabid commanders who spoke of martyrdom's glory. Perhaps the most striking way some Ansar Taliban set themselves apart from their Afghan comrades was by showing a willingness to take heavy casualties to hold ground. When the foreign fighters took ground, they dug in, aiming to keep it, carving trenches and bunkers into the hillsides and laying mines. Afghan Taliban, on the other hand, frequently held territory tenuously, often prepared, in the face of a high body count, to desert positions recently gained. Alliance forces remember Ansar units regularly outmatching them in terms of battlefield skills and weaponry, and the boldness some of them showed in battle unnerved many fighters and commanders in the Alliance's ranks. Rumors abounded at the front of groups of foreign fighters staging mass suicides when on the brink of capture by Alliance forces. Moreover, up-close glimpses Alliance soldiers caught of the lives of foreign fighters deepened their fears.

"Those troops were not like other soldiers," said Atiqullah Baryalai, who commanded the Northern Alliance position opposite the Ansar forces in 2001 during Lindh's months on the front. The foreigners lived in an austerity intimidating even by the standards of Afghan warfare. Baryalai and other Northern Alliance men who fought the foreign Taliban recalled that when Alliance forces would capture an Afghan Taliban position, they would usually find a base with some of the trappings of civilization, like a toilet or collections of books and working kitchens. But the forward Ansar fighters lived like fighting monks.

"If we captured Arab Taliban or Pakistani Taliban bases, it was very dirty," Baryalai remembered, speaking in Kabul in May of 2002. "There was a bad smell. There was no carpet, no furniture."

The goings-on of the Ansar were always a murky matter for the Northern Alliance. On frontline positions, where Afghans faced other Afghans, the two sides would often banter on the radio, trading insults and threats, calling on each other to surrender. Sometimes Baryalai's fighters would raise Ansar troops on the radio and engage in such talk. More often the airwaves carried a silence that underscored the dark mystique surrounding the activities on the other side of the front.

Lindh's unit was part of a bigger Ansar deployment of 2,000 men based mostly in Chichkeh, a village on the Tajik border. From Chichkeh, the foreign fighters fanned out to frontline trenches dug into the grassy slopes on the southern side of the Amu Darya, a shallow river dividing Tajikistan and Afghanistan. The village sits just inside the border of Afghanistan on a terraced plain overlooking a wide valley spread beneath a wall of smoothed peaks marking the Tajik frontier, which stands as the eastern reach of the Tereklitau Mountains. To the south, on the Afghan side of the border, the steppe folds in undulating hills, hard-packed rises covered in the thin grasses that look like dunes frozen in the winter snows that dust the expanse each year.

Abandoned by villagers turned refugees, Chichkeh provided a fallback position for the forwardmost Ansar detachments, which scattered throughout the rolling sweeps to crouch in shallow fox-holes chipped into hillsides laced with landmines. For about a year before September 11, hundreds of Ansar fighters camped in Chichkeh, which is little more than a string of footpaths winding through a few hundred tiny mud huts with empty windows and doors.

The foreign Taliban had taken up mainly in the abandoned village's school and two mosques, one-room mudstones set on cement slabs propped up by rows of cinderblock pillars. "Paradise," reads a charcoal chalking in Arabic on the side wall of one of Chichkeh's mosques, where Ansar fighters bedded on a bare floor, using spent bullet casings pushed into the soft walls as pegs for hanging guns. "In memory of Ansar," reads another etching on an adjacent outside wall. The walls of the schoolhouse and mosques bore many names alongside fighters' jihadi graffiti. "Long Live the Taliban" was written in Dari on one wall of a mosque. "Allah u Akbar," Arabic for "God is great," reads another mosque chalking. "We will continue jihad dead or alive," still another quote in Pashto proclaims.

The area around Chichkeh was pivotal ground since it provided the Northern Alliance river links for supplies and men from Tajikistan. The Taliban had long sought to take the area from the Northern Alliance, which watched with apprehension as the ranks of foreign fighters in the area grew from 2,000 to perhaps as many as 4,000, not including the some 2,000 Pakistanis whom the Alliance regarded as locals of a sort.

As the foreign fighters had increased their numbers at the front in the spring of 2001, the day-to-day slog at the battle lines went on much as usual, with each side trading artillery and machine-gun fire from trenches, some just fifty meters apart. Once every two weeks or so, either the Taliban or the Northern Alliance would launch an attack, shifting the front lines briefly in bloody battles where the death toll often climbed into the hundreds. Any ground taken in advances by either side was normally soon lost, leaving the front for the most part unchanged, deadlocked over a string of trenches running roughly south from the Tajik border around Chichkeh to the Panjshir Valley north of Kabul.

In the summer of 2001, things began to change. Baryalai used locals as spies, eavesdropped on radio traffic among foreign fighters, and occasionally received intelligence leaks from the Pakistani army to develop a picture of Ansar's plans, which increasingly seemed geared toward a large-scale offensive. Alliance commanders like Baryalai knew that a successful Taliban push along the northern edge of the Takhar front could cripple their forces and perhaps crush their toehold on Afghanistan altogether. Alliance defense strategists at the time suspected an imminent Taliban assault led by the foreign fighters aimed at taking the borderlands around the river, a move that would fold the Northern Alliance lines to the south and east and force a retreat. All possible retreat routes would have left the Northern Alliance cut from its supply lines to the north, leaving them to weaken gradually in a pocket surrounded by Taliban forces. Faced with a potentially ruinous defeat, they planned an offensive of their own meant to retake the whole of Takhar province. Such a move called for enough force to seize and hold all the lands west of Taloqan. In the months before September 11, Baryalai fortified the front with new weapons and recruits who had been drilling intensively, matching the Taliban buildup.

Around the time Lindh's unit took up positions on their hills, foreign fighters elsewhere on the front were launching heavy attacks almost daily, forcing the Northern Alliance to bear down in defensive positions and fight to hold the ground they had with little hope of making gains with their own attacks.

With the front dangling on the brink of a major clash, assassins posing as television journalists detonated a bomb hidden in their camera as they met with Ahmed Shah Massoud for a staged interview. The main leader of the Northern Alliance against the Taliban died on September 9, 2001, his assassination a harbinger of bloodier events to come.

Word of Massoud's death seemed to embolden the attacking foreign fighters, who intensified assaults on Alliance positions, though without making any significant gains. With Massoud slain and his forces pinned down in defensive positions, the momentum of the battle seemed to be shifting in the Taliban's favor as they pressed harder and harder to break the Alliance.

Then came September 11, a day that Baryalai and other Alliance commanders immediately knew would reshape everything. Within weeks of the terrorist attacks on America, the White House began sounding the death knell for the Taliban because of its support for bin Laden. And Pakistan's longtime support for the Taliban abruptly ended when Pervez Musharraf declared his allegiance to the United States in its efforts against terrorism.

Baryalai and other Alliance commanders knew their moment had come and watched as the Taliban attacks trickled off, with the frontline fighters along Takhar holding back in anticipation of the real fight to come, the one that would bring Americans onto battlefields hitherto long forgotten in the West.

C☪

Lindh heard the news of September 11 by word of mouth from others in his unit who listened to radio broadcasts. With no access to a radio himself, much less to a television or newspaper, Lindh was unsure what to think of the attacks and the speculation that bin Laden was behind them. In any case, Lindh perceived bin Laden and any conflict he had with America as separate from the Taliban's fight against the Northern Alliance.

Lindh knew that the United States had launched cruise missiles aimed at bin Laden into jihadi camps around Khost and Jalalabad in August of 1998 in retaliation for the embassy attacks in East Africa. He thought the United States might strike in such a way again somewhere inside Afghanistan in an effort to kill bin Laden, but he did not imagine that the United States would attack the Taliban itself for supporting bin Laden. Lindh was tragically wrong in many ways.

Shortly after September 11, President George W. Bush publicly announced that suspected terrorists were no longer America's only targets; countries that supported and harbored terrorists would face military action as well. Bush first singled out Afghanistan as America's principal enemy. News of the U.S. policy shift never made it to the remote hillsides where Lindh continued his tour of guard duty.

In the weeks that followed September 11, life at the front for Lindh went on much as it had before, although a heady tension was settling over the area. Shortly after the attacks, bin Laden had closed his camps and sent some of the hands from al-Farooq and elsewhere to the front. A trainer from al-Farooq named Hakeem, whom Lindh had seen in bin Laden's entourage, showed

up suddenly at Lindh's position in early October. Hakeem talked
boastfully to anyone who would listen about bin Laden, claiming
the Saudi had organized the attacks and that the Americans were
going after him.

Hakeem's claims, which Lindh questioned, meant something
unsettling for Lindh. The moral, ethical, and religious reasoning
that had drawn Lindh and others to fight in the trenches against
fellow Islamic believers in Afghanistan did not call for attacks like
those unleashed on September 11. And whatever misconceptions
Lindh had about bin Laden, one thing was clear: the Taliban was
supporting him. Many of the foreign fighters in the trenches
alongside Lindh began to question the Taliban and its support of
bin Laden as sketchy details about the thousands of civilian casualties reached them in their remote post.

Some considered defecting, looking for ways to flee Takhar.
But the U.S. airstrikes that had begun in the south on October 7
had frozen all transportation to and from the north. Slipping away
on foot seemed out of the question. A walk back to the nearest
town of any size, Konduz, would take more than two days over
frigid steppe supposedly roamed by bandits. There seemed to be
no way out, so Lindh never really considered abandoning his position, even when warplanes began attacking the area. Lindh
watched from his hillside as bombers raked targets along the front
beginning in November. He was still unsure about what was happening. He thought perhaps the United States was retaliating in-
discriminately since bombs seemed to be falling on both sides of
the front line. He had no idea that, in fact, the Northern Alliance
was helping to guide some of the falling bombs.

On the opposite side of the front lines, Baryalai and other Al-
liance commanders had grown frustrated and impatient through
September and October, especially since they had hoped to see
U.S. planes soften the Taliban positions enough to break the front

before cold weather froze the battlefield for the winter. The Alliance commanders used the time wisely, though, to make ready a siege of territory in Afghanistan far larger than they had hoped for only months before. They knew that when the front line in Takhar broke, all of northern Afghanistan would open to them.

When the Americans finally did begin targeting the Taliban holding the front lines against the Northern Alliance, the Taliban initially seemed resolute. Wave after wave of bombs along the hilly front kicked up huge clouds of dust that would clear to reveal Taliban fighters, who had crouched in bunkers, standing once again on hilltops, shouting and firing their weapons into the air towards U.S. planes in a show of defiance. Their bravado was short lived, as the United States shifted its tactics from blanket bombings with B-52s to pinpoint strikes with fighter jets, which rocketed Taliban positions with more lethal effect.

Atiqullah Baryalai worked with U.S. forces that had arrived at the front in Takhar to point out the positions of bin Laden's foreign legions, the American target of choice. Lindh's unit was stationed far enough back so that bombs never hit his hillside post, but the airstrikes were breaking up Taliban positions elsewhere along the front, forcing Lindh's brigade to fall back in order to keep up a rear guard. Lindh left his orange sack at his position on the hill, thinking his unit might regroup and eventually return to the area. But as they moved away from their posts, the entire front line folded, and all the Taliban in the area broke into a full retreat toward Konduz.

Swelling to about one hundred men, Lindh's group fled on foot as the Northern Alliance overran their positions. The Alliance soldiers had a retreating army in front of them and quickly set to killing any stragglers who could not reach the safety of Konduz, where Taliban forces routed from Mazar-i-Sharif, Taloqan, and elsewhere in northern Afghanistan were rallying for what appeared to be a last stand.

CHAPTER SIX

An Uncertain Surrender

KONDUZ is a shady farm town with rows of thick, leafy trees lining wide dirt streets, where the dusty air jingles with the bells of horse-drawn carts and smells of freshly cut wood, unwashed onions, and gasoline for the tractors that come and go from the outlying wheat fields. On a normal day, the street scenes give Konduz the appearance of a quaint old world, broken down and dirtied by modern poverty. The horse carts, brightly decorated with puffballs colored red and blue, number as many as the cars, which range from vintage Soviet models to the latest Japanese off-road truck.

Under Taliban control, Konduz became a garrison town, a central stronghold for forces deployed all over Takhar and Mazar-i-Sharif. Taliban commanders used large school compounds they closed to house their troops and parked their heavy armor at the Konduz arsenal. Foreign fighters were a common sight in the streets, where they would walk together in small groups through the bazaars.

After the Northern Alliance had routed the Taliban from Mazar-i-Sharif and Takhar, the ousted fighters swarmed Konduz, thronging the school bases and madrassas. Residents, who had long chafed under Taliban control, grew terrified, as did the Taliban who saw the Northern Alliance gradually surrounding the town and sealing them off. The Taliban set up a city perimeter to hold off a siege and ordered all the residents to stay indoors as a standoff unfolded. Virtually everyone either fled the city or obeyed the order to stay inside, leaving the local population largely without an eye on what was happening outside.

Lindh's group straggled into the increasing confusion of Konduz after walking virtually nonstop for about three days, trekking over fifty miles of rolling desert terrain scattered with the bones of dead sheep and goats amid the rubble of farming villages. At night on the wasted steppe, the temperature dropped so low that Lindh and his comrades had to keep marching simply to stay warm. They had left virtually everything behind, abandoning all provisions in their retreat, bringing nothing to sustain them as they marched. They dared not stop to forage or rest for fear of being taken by the Alliance troops who roamed the hills in jeeps and trucks.

Lindh grew extremely weak during the retreat. Freezing and exhausted, he could hardly form words. His heart seemed to thump erratically in his chest, which ached heavily as dehydration and hunger worsened his fatigue. His stomach twisted in pain with another bout of the food poisoning that had sickened him in Kandahar. Soon he could walk only with the help of his comrades, who carried him as he limped along, while others collapsed and were left behind. During one of the evenings of the retreat, Lindh, still fading, thought he was going to die when a group of Uzbek Taliban fighters approached them in the winter gloom. Lindh's group thought the Uzbeks were Alliance troops, and a fierce fight broke out, killing more than thirty of the men in Lindh's brigade. Lindh narrowly escaped and managed to stagger on to Konduz. His Ansar comrades there shuttered him in a safe house with other Arabic speakers, where he remained for days as the siege outside intensified.

Forced indoors, most of the residents in Konduz only had

fleeting looks at the Taliban foreigners as the retreating fighters poured into the city. Even in years past during the war, Konduz residents had little close contact with the foreign fighters, who came and went from the area, as Lindh's unit had, escorted by the Taliban with an air of secrecy. Only a handful of ranking Afghan Taliban ever dealt directly with the foreign fighters, who remained darkly mysterious to virtually everyone outside their circle as they traveled through Afghanistan shrouded in myth. But doctors at the Konduz hospital in the center of town got an up-close look at Ansar's soldiers during the siege that none is soon to forget, a telling encounter that left little doubt about the nature of the men bin Laden's camps turned out.

A group of foreign fighters who arrived in Konduz from Takhar about the time Lindh entered the city went immediately to the area hospital, where they carried in dozens of badly wounded men caught under American bombs. While Konduz's streets were tense and quiet, the halls of the hospital were bloody and chaotic. The broken fighters bore some of the worst injuries any of the doctors had seen, even through decades of treating war casualties. The gaping stomach wounds of some men dripped blood and bile. Crushed arms hung bloody and ragged off some men, while others were missing arms and legs altogether. Some of the fighters had head injures that left their skulls partially shattered, exposing their living brains.

"When the U.S. planes broke the Takhar front line, things became crazy in Konduz," said Professor Aziz Ullah, the head of the Konduz hospital. Ullah saw the first group of foreign fighters to arrive at the hospital early in the morning, roughly two days after the front lines in Takhar folded. About six men came limping to the gates carrying wounded comrades. A young dentist on Ullah's staff, Dr. Haji Mohammad Packdill, was leaving work after being sent home sick and was walking towards the hospital's garden gates as the foreign fighters entered. A fighter apparently in charge of the small band began shouting at Packdill and then turned his gun on him. Ullah saw the scene from his office and rushed into the courtyard, but arrived too late. The fighter shot Packdill once in the stomach, watching him fall to his knees clutching his wound before kicking him over and firing two more shots into his head and back. The fighter then took aim at Ullah as he rushed toward Packdill and pulled the trigger, but the gun jammed. Then the fighter began shouting, demanding emergency care for the wounded men and threatening to kill any doctors who refused. "They were ready to kill us all," Ullah said. "I felt like I had been taken prisoner in my own hospital."

The fighter spoke Russian, said he was Chechen, and more like him soon followed. Groups of ten and twenty trickled into the hospital throughout the day, until wounded fighters filled all the beds, spilling into the hallways. Numbering roughly 120, the fighters remained suspicious of the doctors, accusing them of being sympathetic to the Northern Alliance and threatening to kill any so-called traitors. Uninjured fighters stood fully armed over the doctors as they worked in the emergency room, threatening to kill any medic who moved too slowly among the patients. The fighters ordered the doctors to hurry, at one point telling surgeons to not bother washing instruments between patients.

"We didn't think they were human," said Dr. Zafar Noori, chief of surgery at the hospital. "They acted like they were raised by animals." Ullah added, "Have you ever heard of anyone bringing a Kalashnikov into an operating room?"

By the end of the day, some two hundred wounded fighters were laid out in the hospital. Most of the injured were Pakistanis, who were able to communicate with the doctors somewhat in Pashto or Dari. About half could only stare vacantly when spoken to in local languages or English, leaving the medics to surmise

that most of the men hailed from the Arab world or perhaps somewhere farther away. The group held the hospital for two weeks as
the standoff around Konduz wore on.

☪

Though they had the city surrounded, Northern Alliance commanders did not want to march on Konduz for fear of unleashing
a fight in the populated area that could kill as many civilians as
soldiers. And the Taliban knew they could not fight their way
through the Alliance lines outside the city to make a break for
Kandahar, especially given the presence of U.S. warplanes over-
head that had already smashed retreating columns of trucks moving from Mazar-i-Sharif to Konduz. So the two sides began laby-
rinthine and disorganized surrender talks, which led to a split
Northern Alliance leadership talking to different factions of the
surrounded Taliban.

Gen. Rashid Dostum, a longtime strongman in northern Afghanistan whose forces, along with Tajik Mohammed Atta, had
recently retaken Mazar-i-Sharif, negotiated a deal with Taliban
commander Mullah Fazel and regional governor Mullah Nuri.
Dostum had returned to Afghanistan from exile in Turkey in
April 2001 to renew a fight against the Taliban in his old territory.
Fazel, the commander of the Taliban's army in the north, was his
chief rival and was loath to give up to the Uzbek, who was by
then backed by U.S. Special Forces.

With Konduz in a standoff, Dostum and Fazel began several
days of talks by radio and then met face to face twice, first at Dostum's newly reclaimed garrison outside Mazar-i-Sharif and then
again on the outskirts of Konduz during the final days of the
siege. The American intelligence officers and Special Forces
troops on hand with the Alliance forces kept away from the talks,
which seemed to be breaking down in the face of Fazel's initial

defiance. But any Taliban hopes of holding off an advance on Konduz by American-backed Alliance forces faded quickly when U.S. AC-130 gunships flew in to pound Taliban positions one night late in the siege. The next day, Taliban commanders struck a deal with Dostum. They agreed to turn over the foreign fighters to his forces, who planned to jail them indefinitely and perhaps put them on trial either in Afghanistan or in an international court. The rest of the Afghan Taliban were to be jailed initially, but later freed.

At Fazel's word, Taliban commanders ordered a group of foreign fighters to form a convoy that was to be the first of several group surrenders. Among the four hundred foreign Taliban chosen for that first handover was Pakistani volunteer Enamul Hak, who remembered seeing Lindh in the group too.

Hak had waited out the Konduz siege with hundreds of other fighters, mostly Pakistanis, holed up in one of the larger area madrassas. The Pakistanis had been ordered by their Afghan commanders to remain hidden, since the presence of foreign fighters among the Taliban in Konduz was a major hitch in the surrender talks. Dostum and other Alliance commanders like Atiqullah Baryalai were willing to let the Afghan Taliban lay down their arms and resume life without fear of prison or reprisal. There was to be no such amnesty for the foreigners, whom many in the Alliance ranks wanted to see executed for their suspected role in killing Massoud. Lindh, Hak, and other foreign fighters had heard about the surrender deal from Taliban commanders, who told them to join the first convoy, without explaining, apparently, that they were to be jailed indefinitely by Dostum. The Afghan Taliban leaders had effectively sold out the foreign fighters, leading them to believe that they would be disarmed and allowed to pass unharmed on to Herat, while knowing Dostum had agreed to no such thing.

At that time, the Taliban still controlled Herat. Lindh thought that once he got to Herat he would find transportation to Bannu, where he would get his belongings, before heading back to the United States to see his family. The Taliban were uneasy, despite the deal. Dostum seemed more likely to be lenient with the foreign fighters than Massoud's lieutenants, but the beefy Uzbek warlord was far from a safe bet. Dostum had a fearsome reputation known well by Lindh and others in the surrendering group. Dostum reportedly enjoys medieval-style public executions of enemy prisoners and traitor soldiers with a modern twist, such as tying them to the treads of tanks and grinding them into the ground. A few weeks earlier, Dostum and his men had struck fear into the Taliban ranks during their capture of Mazar-i-Sharif, where Dostum's forces slaughtered roughly one hundred Taliban fighters who had holed up in a schoolhouse.

Despite what Taliban commanders had told the surrendering troops, Dostum's terms called for the foreign fighters to drive themselves from Konduz to the edge of Mazar-i-Sharif, where they were to be disarmed and then jailed at Dostum's fortress, called Qala-i-Jangi. Dostum had no intention of letting the foreign Taliban pass through his territory, but some in the group, like Lindh, thought that the deal would allow them to leave Mazar-i-Sharif after handing over their weapons. Some in the group even had notions of traveling safely to Kandahar. Still others had ideas about fighting on. Three of the trucks in the convoy were loaded with arms and ammunition.

☪

Around November 24, 2001, still weak from the Takhar retreat, Lindh wearily climbed into the bed of one of the heavy trucks in the convoy, as the rest of the group loaded up the seven other trucks and as many more Toyota off-road pickups. Under a cold and clear morning sky, the trucks grumbled to a start and began moving out. The convoy jostled inch by inch over beaten road trailing through the hills, kicking up clouds of fine dust.

The road from Konduz turns down, dropping off a short plateau to curve through a barren ridge opening to a colorless steppe, a route traveled mostly by nomads, thieves, and fighters, home only to lizards and vultures. Along the way the trucks passed half a dozen shattered Soviet tanks and twice as many obliterated Taliban pickups that had been rocketed by U.S. planes. Northern Alliance vehicles packed with fighters rode on every side of the convoy, with the Afghans nervously aiming their guns at the foreign Taliban. The trucks rumbled without stopping through the few mud brick villages along the way, tiny clusters of cracked houses that seemed to be sinking into the weedy, packed sands. The vacant horizon beyond stretched across hazy distances ruled with lines of stripped telephone poles, disused and falling down like bare crosses.

When the trucks finally neared Mazar-i-Sharif, about six hours after leaving Konduz, the Alliance troops brought them to a halt along a strip of blacktop road not far from the city airstrip. The Alliance forces wanted to disarm the group before it entered Mazar-i-Sharif for fear the foreigners could stage a fight in the city center where civilians would be caught in the crossfire. Veteran Northern Alliance commander Haji Raof was in charge of the forces on hand when the convoy halted on a curve of the road, where the surrendering Taliban were ordered down from their trucks. As they leapt from the convoy, some seemed to be rejecting the notion of surrender. "They were all acting differently," Raof said. "Some of them were scared. Some of them were angry. Some of them were ready to fight."

A group of Taliban immediately formed a loose firing line, facing off with Northern Alliance guards, who quickly massed at the top of the road aiming their own guns from about three hundred meters away. The Taliban in the group ready to fight had a plan to retake Mazar-i-Sharif. They hoped to storm the airfield outside the city and hold it long enough for Taliban reinforcements to arrive from Balkh, about ten miles west. Since the bulk of the Alliance troops were centered on Konduz, the plotters thought that the "surrendering" force was capable of capturing and holding the airfield while the rest of Mazar-i-Sharif could be taken relatively easily with Taliban reinforcements. In Raof's opinion, "They came to fight. They wanted to die."

That was fine with Raof, who sent a handful of his men to walk over to the Taliban side with a simple message: If you want to fight it out here, you will all be killed. "When they saw that there were a lot more of our guys, they said 'okay,'" Raof said. The Northern Alliance fighters behind Raof clearly outnumbered the some four hundred Taliban. With no signs of Taliban reinforcements in sight as Raof's men bore down on the convoy, the group leaders decided to bide their time. They sent word back that they would drop their guns in a pile by the side of the road before climbing back into the trucks and driving on to Mazar-i-Sharif. Some still appeared reluctant, and there seemed to be confusion about who was in charge and what, exactly, they had all agreed to.

Raof's men supervised the Taliban fighters as they piled their weapons on the roadside and got back into the trucks. The Alliance soldiers didn't search their captives, and many pocketed grenades, pistols, and knives. Some of the prisoners faked injuries and hid weapons beneath their bandages. Others managed to withhold weapons as large even as Kalashnikovs in the small of their backs under loose winter clothes. Raof's men didn't search the fighters well partly because they didn't want to offend their fellow Muslim captives by suggesting they were untrustworthy.

But the biggest reason was that they were scared to go near these foreign fighters, men with a reputation for suicidal fanaticism unheard of among Afghans. And so the convoy started up again, loaded with many still-armed Taliban, some of whom hoped to strike a blow against the Northern Alliance.

☪

Rolling into Mazar-i-Sharif, the trucks passed the weathered blue domes of the city's namesake shrine, the tomb of Hazrat Ali, where flocks of white pigeons swirl above crowds of beggars and amputees always on the grounds and in the surrounding bazaar. As the prisoners watched from the moving trucks, the city's broken-down buildings, brushed with milky blue paint, fell away when the convoy turned toward the farming flats surrounding Dostum's prison compound, Qala-i-Jangi.

Sitting amid sweeping wheat fields, Qala-i-Jangi's mass of sloped, crenellated walls looks as though it were hewn from a low, outer rise of the Alborz Range, the treeless hills knuckling the steppe southwest of Mazar-i-Sharif. Built in 1895, the fortress looks like a bizarre mix of primeval and modern war gloom hulking over an enclosed area about as long and wide as a stadium. Antennae, heavy machine guns, and razor wire sit atop mud-wall ramparts and dry moats that look as though they were built to fend off Mongol hordes, rather than tank columns or airstrikes. Tilted poles run electric wires over the antiquated walls, feeding voltage to contemporary accouterments like radios and satellite phones, which even third-world militias like the Taliban would not be without. The road into the fort winds through a cluster of farmhouses that knot around the fortress gate, a high arching entrance of poured concrete that looks out of place alongside the mudstone. Inside, the main drive rolls through a parade ground scattered with a collection of vehicles, heavy guns, and provisions laid out randomly in front of the main fortress building, a concrete bunker complex built into the side of the outer wall.

Lindh's convoy motored through the fortress's outer gates, past two squat cannons sitting idle at the entrance, traversing the main grounds and continuing through a second set of gates, into the inner yard of a walled-off back quarter. For some of the fighters in the convoy, arriving at the fortress was a homecoming. Many of the Uzbek fighters in the Ansar brigade had trained at the fortress as recently as two months before, when the Taliban controlled the area. The Uzbeks knew that much of the arms the Taliban had stored there were likely still piled in the armory, unlocked rooms ringing the inside of the separate back area next to where the trucks had come to a stop.

Winter's early darkness was inking the sky as the convoy halted. Alliance commanders had hoped to get the trucks all the way to the only proper jail in the area, an aging prison about eighty miles west of Mazar-i-Sharif in Sheberghan. However, they decided to stop at the fortress overnight because no one wanted to be on the road after dark with several truckloads of foreign fighters. The only place Alliance soldiers had to put the prisoners as dusk fell was in an unused basement beneath a pink bunker house in the back area, the sole confined space Dostum's men could effectively guard. Even having them out in the open yard inside the fortress walls was thought by Sayed Kamel, Dostum's chief of security, to be risky. "I was telling them to hurry because it was getting late and that the prisoners should be kept in separate rooms overnight," Kamel said.

Kamel and a group of Alliance commanders watched nervously as the prisoners began to descend from the trucks. Things went wrong immediately. One of the first captives off the trucks strode over to the group of commanders, throwing himself at their feet, clutching an armed grenade to his chest. The prisoner looked up at the surprised men, catching their eyes for a moment before the blast. Kamel dove for cover and shouted for the others to do the same, but they moved too slowly. The grenade went off, killing two Alliance commanders, severely wounding a third, and tearing the suicide attacker's body nearly in half.

The blast set off a momentary panic, but quickly the Alliance guards regained control and began herding the captives into the basement hold of the pink building. Originally, they had planned to search each prisoner carefully before sending him into the cells, but the attack and the darkening skies forced the Alliance guards to drive the group en masse below ground, knowing then that many still carried arms.

Lindh was shocked at the attack, which violated the surrender agreement as he understood it. Still, he remained hopeful that the group would be allowed to travel on to Herat. Pushed down by Dostum's men, Lindh and his four hundred other comrades filled the dark basement's seven cramped rooms, where a din of voices speaking in no less than a dozen different languages echoed off the dank cement walls. Wounded captives filled three of the rooms, while in other cells groups of fighters huddled together wondering what would happen next.

As Lindh rested in one of the rooms, a grenade came tumbling down a small air vent high in the wall, killing several prisoners and wounding many others when it exploded amid a group of captives. The grenade was a goodnight kiss from Alliance fighters angered by the earlier attack. The blast narrowly missed Lindh, who spent the rest of the night crouching on the dirt floor near a corner used as a toilet because there was no room to lie down anywhere else. Sometime during the night, word spread throughout the basement that Dostum was still going to allow the Taliban to continue on to Herat, despite the confusion surrounding the grenade attack and the reprisal bomb tossed into the basement.

Dostum's men even sent down plates of rice as a sort of peace offering.

But some of the prisoners wanted nothing to do with Dostum's pacts. Enamul Hak, the Pakistani Taliban who saw Lindh climb into the convoy in Konduz, huddled with some of his fellow countrymen in the basement early on and watched nervously as a group of Arabs and Uzbeks began talking about how they might yet have a chance to fight their way out.

According to Hak and another Pakistani Talib in the basement that night, Wahid Ahmad, the group of four hundred was split. The Pakistanis were willing to chance a surrender deal in the hopes of being returned home, but the foreign fighters from Arab countries and elsewhere wanted to fight. The Pakistanis, for the most part, felt they had fairly good odds of being returned at some point across the nearby border and that they likely faced no troubles at home, because Pakistani authorities had long backed the Taliban.

The foreign fighters from other countries had no such hopes. Most came from lands where the Taliban and al-Qaida were loathed and affiliation with them would be punishable by death, or worse. Better to die a martyr at Qala-i-Jangi, some thought, than to be tortured and executed at home. The Uzbeks in particular seemed ready to take their chances fighting rather than remain in the hands of Dostum, who, himself an Uzbek, was said to take special delight in the torture of ethnic brethren who had chosen to fight against him.

The night in the basement passed quickly, with disorganized groups clustered in various rooms in different bands according to nationality. As dawn broke, no consensus seemed to have been reached as to how to proceed with the surrender.

CHAPTER SEVEN

Jihad's Last Cry

AS THE sun rose on the chilly morning of November 25, Northern Alliance guards descended to the basement to begin bringing up the prisoners for interrogation. The first of the captives left the basement as ordered, allowed themselves to be searched and bound, and were led to a strip of ground on the side of the building facing the fort's stables where they sat waiting to be questioned by two CIA officers. At about ten in the morning, after some two hundred prisoners had left the basement without incident, Lindh too mounted the metal stairs leading from the cellar. At the top of the steps, two Alliance guards searched him and tied his elbows behind his back before seating him with the other prisoners slumped in rows by the side of the building. Alliance guards walked among the bound detainees, occasionally kicking and beating them with sticks. Many still suffered wounds and moaned loudly in the open air. At one point, as Lindh sat motionless, one of Dostum's guards struck him in the head, leaving him dazed as he watched two men who appeared to be Americans question prisoners one by one.

Lindh thought the two Americans were somehow under the command of Dostum, because Afghan guards aided them and took orders from them. It seemed to Lindh that the two Americans must have seen the guards beating the prisoners randomly, but neither appeared concerned. Lindh began to fear that if identified as an American he would be separated from the group and kept behind in Dostum's custody for further questioning. Lindh dreaded the idea of remaining in Qala-i-Jangi, where he expected to be tortured and killed by Dostum's men.

The Americans Lindh saw were CIA operatives Mike Spann and Dave Tyson. During the early interrogations, an Iraqi prisoner had told Spann that there was an Irishman among the prisoners. Spann noticed Lindh in the group and was told the disheveled fighter, whose skin was lighter than most, had been overheard speaking English. Lindh also drew the attention of an Afghan camera man, who began videotaping Lindh, providing an eerie record of one of the most compelling moments of the war — two Americans face to face in a remote corner of Afghanistan, each there for reasons of personal conviction, yet on opposite sides of battle lines.

"Hey, you, right here with your head down," Spann called to Lindh as he sat limply among the other prisoners. "Look at me; I know you speak English," Spann said, eyeing Lindh as he sat unresponsive. "Look at me. Where did you get the British military sweater?"

Northern Alliance guards hauled Lindh to his feet and shoved him over to a blanket spread over the dirt, where he kneeled and sagged his head, letting his long brown hair fall over his face. Spann squatted at the edge of the rug facing the prisoner as the rest of the captives and guards looked on.

"Where are you from?" Spann said. "You believe in what you're doing here that much, you're willing to be killed here? How were you recruited to come here? Who brought you here? Hey!"

Spann snapped twice in the prisoner's face but still got no response.

"What's your name?" Spann continued. "Hey, who brought

you here? Wake up! Who brought you here to Afghanistan? How did you get here?"

Spann matched Lindh's silence for a moment, looking him over in a long pause as a distant autumn sun rose and warmed the chill morning air. They couldn't have appeared more different sitting silently opposite each other as the muted clatter of Qala-i-Jangi's troops, trucks, and horses stirred the hush between them. Square-jawed, with a neatly trimmed mustache, Spann was built like a brick house. The brawn in his chest and shoulders showed through even the heavy fleece he wore with his jeans. Lindh by this point looked like a wasted waif, rake thin under a sweater of his own, draped heavily over tattered traditional Afghan clothes that resembled dirty pajamas.

"What, are you puzzled?" asked Spann, who dropped to his knees on the rug and took aim at Lindh with a digital camera.

"Put your head up," Spann said. "Don't make me have to get them to hold your head up. Push your hair back. Push your hair back so I can see your face."

Lindh glowered and hunched angrily until a nearby Afghan guard reached over, pulled his hair back and held his head up for Spann's camera. Spann might have been surprised by the face, which looked young and smooth under a silky brown beard that matched the color of his wide, almost girlish eyes. But the angry expression of defiance and humiliation Lindh wore Spann had undoubtedly seen on the others he had already questioned.

"You got to talk to me," Spann said. "All I want to do is talk to you and find out what your story is. I know you speak English."

Lindh said nothing, and Spann clearly displayed frustration when Tyson walked over to see what was up.

"He won't talk to me," Spann said.

"Okay, all right," Tyson said. "We explained what the deal is to him."

"I was explaining to the guy we just want to talk to him, find out what his story is," Spann said.

"Well, he's a Muslim, you know," Tyson said, lowering his voice for a moment to talk quietly with Spann before going on to speak loudly enough so Lindh was sure to hear.

"The problem is he needs to decide if he wants to live or die, and die here," Tyson said. "If he don't want to die here, he's gonna die here. We're just going to leave him, and he's going to fucking sit in prison the rest of his fucking short life. It's his decision, man. We can only help the guys who want to talk to us. We can only get the Red Cross to help so many guys. If they don't talk to us, we can't—"

"Do you know the people here you're working with are terrorists, and killed other Muslims?" Spann interrupted, turning from Tyson to Lindh suddenly. "There were several hundred Muslims killed in the bombing in New York City. Is that what the Koran teaches? I don't think so. Are you going to talk to us?"

"That's all right, man," Tyson said. "Gotta give him a chance, he got his chance."

Indeed, Lindh had his chance, but he wasn't taking it with Americans. Instead, he silently chose to risk death with his Taliban comrades, a choice he had made before and was to make again several times over. It never struck Lindh, apparently, that Spann, as a fellow American, could help him return home. Foolishly, he still hoped that somehow the group would be freed and allowed to leave the fortress peacefully after the interrogations. Lindh hoped that he might be mistaken for a light-skinned Pakistani, lumped in with other Pakistanis and let go.

"Did you get a chance to look at any of the passports?" Spann asked Tyson as they turned away from Lindh.

"There's a couple of Saudis, and I didn't see the others," Tyson said.

"I wonder what this guy's got," Spann said, motioning to Lindh.

Spann still had no idea Lindh was an American as a guard pulled Lindh to his feet and shoved him to an area with the other previously interrogated prisoners. And he didn't live long enough to find out what the rest of the world would soon know. The shorter of their two lives turned out to be Spann's.

Forgetting Lindh, Spann began interrogating other Taliban prisoners brought up from their basement cells. Northern Alliance guards continued searching, tethering, and lining up prisoners in the yard. About half an hour later, as Alliance guards called into the cellar for another prisoner, as many as half a dozen, mostly Uzbeks, suddenly rounded the steps, tossing grenades, yelling "Allah u Akbar!" The guards fired into the crush of prisoners charging up the stairs, but were soon overpowered as more men leapt up from behind them and fought towards the outside door. In a second, a revolt was on.

Seated by the side of the building, Lindh heard the sounds of shots and screams and rose to his feet as some of the prisoners around him began shouting and untying each other. He turned to run but was shot in the leg as Alliance fighters standing on the roof of the pink building fired Kalashnikovs down into the yard, spraying the scattering prisoners. As the gunfire quickened, Lindh lay bleeding, motionless where he fell, watching the bloody scene unfold. All around Lindh in those opening moments of the uprising, prisoners trying to flee shuddered and fell to the ground in bloody heaps, their bodies shredded by machine gun fire, many with their hands still bound behind their backs. He and another wounded prisoner lay in the yard playing dead for the duration of the fourteen-hour shootout.

Across the yard, at the opening sounds of the revolt, Spann and Tyson turned to face a crush of prisoners sweeping toward them as the fighting spread out from the basement building. The group headed for Spann, who, in his jeans and sweater, offered a more obvious target than Tyson, who wore native dress and a beard. Both men pulled pistols and opened fire into the horde rushing Spann, who shot one coming at him dead while Tyson gunned down another. But still more were on their feet fanning out through the yard and moving in on Spann, who managed to gun down two more before the prisoners swept over him, tearing at his skin, kicking and beating him as he went down to become the first American casuality in Afghanistan. Tyson rushed to where Spann had fallen and called out, but got no answer as Spann lay unmoving on his back under a pile of freshly dead bodies, apparently Spann's last kills in the moments before his own death.

As Tyson drew nearer to Spann, a Talib ran from the basement firing a pistol tilted to the side gangland-style, blasting at Tyson from roughly ten feet away. Tyson spun around and emptied his own high-powered Browning into the fighter, dropping him. Tyson then holstered his handgun and reached for Spann's Kalashnikov, pulling it from the hands of a dead prisoner, who had managed to pry it from Spann during their struggle. By now, most of the prisoners had managed to free their hands and were on their feet, advancing as Alliance guards ran from the yard. Tyson made his way out too, pumping rifle rounds into the mob as he backpedaled to the gate, and ran for cover in the fort's main building.

The retreating Alliance troops began shooting into the prison's inner yard from atop the fort's high walls as the freed fighters seized the armory, a row of storage sheds along the inner yard's northern wall, filled with Kalashnikovs, grenades, mortars, rocket launchers, and ammunition. In moments, the prisoners were better armed than they had been before dumping their weapons by the side of the road outside Mazar-i-Sharif.

Armed again, the insurgent Taliban seemed crazed with suicidal abandon. A group stormed the stables, where Dostum kept
his prized cavalry of about forty horses. They leapt onto the
steeds bareback, bursting from the makeshift barn, only to be cut
down by Alliance guns that killed the horses and riders alike. A
few climbed into the twin row of fir trees that lined the yard's
drive and used the evergreen needles as cover for a sniper's view
of Alliance fighters. More Taliban ran up the walls along the western edge of the yard and began to inch toward the Alliance positions on the eastern side. Another group took control of the inner
yard's gates and seemed poised to charge into the outer courtyard,
towards the fort's main building, where Tyson and a group of
German journalists remained pinned down. Heavy fire from Alliance positions on the northeast walls forced the Ansar fighters to
fall back to the western side of the yard, leaving the basement
building next to which Lindh lay in the middle of a massive gun
battle that lasted past nightfall, when Lindh's Taliban comrades
dragged him into the basement.

Outside the prison compound, Gen. Faqir Mohammad, one of
Dostum's commanders, feared that if the prisoners held ground
by the inner yard's gatehouse, they could fight their way into the
outer yard and soon gain control of the entire fort. To push them
back, he ordered in three tanks, which ground up fallen bodies
under their tracks as they formed a blockade and opened fire on
the stables and high parapets the prisoners were using for cover.
The huge guns booming at close range shook the grounds, but the
Taliban answered with rocket-propelled grenades seized from the
armory. The prisoners eventually forced Alliance tanks to roll
back under fire from their own stolen armaments. Now Alliance
forces began massing on the outside of the fort as well, taking
shots at any prisoners who left cover on the walls and gunning
down those who tried to escape the battle by leaping into the dry

moat outside. Many more of the Alliance troops idled behind cover or hid altogether, shaken and frightened, waiting for help.

The foreigners, now in complete control of the inner yard, made little effort to abandon what was clearly a suicide mission, fighting with a grim disregard for their own lives that dismayed Dostum's Afghans. Occasionally, one prisoner might pause over the dead body of another, wailing, crying for the good fortune of the martyred soldier destined for eternal bliss honoring battlefield sacrifice. More commonly, however, Alliance fighters who took part in the battle remember being horrified as they watched prisoners pulling weapons from the hands of fallen comrades without bothering to check for a pulse.

During the opening confusion of the revolt, Tyson had lost his backpack and all the communications equipment it contained. Fortunately, one of the journalists carried a satellite phone. Tyson used it to call for help at the U.S. Embassy in Tashkent, which relayed the message to the coalition command at a schoolhouse in Mazar-i-Sharif. Having gotten Tyson's message, U.S. and British troops arrived at the fortress later in the afternoon as the fighting continued to spin further out of control. Coalition troops quickly joined local fighters at a position atop the gatehouse. British forces set up heavy machine guns that hammered the inner yard, providing cover as a radio operator set up equipment to communicate with U.S. warplanes en route to the area.

Four U.S. Special Forces troops set out to free Tyson and the journalists, braving mortar fire to take up gunning positions in the outer courtyard near the main building, where they held off Taliban fire long enough for the group to slip over a wall to safety outside the fortress. Spann was thought dead, however, and there was no way to reach his body because of the heavy gunfire crisscrossing the inner yard.

Within hours of the revolt's first shots, two U.S. fighter planes appeared in the sky, circling Qala-i-Jangi, waiting for a ground command to fire. Alliance Gen. Majid Rozi told the Special Forces troops to rocket a white single-story building next to the pink house seized by the Ansar fighters. Americans radioed coordinates to the airborne fighters, and moments later a silver dart flashed out of the sky with a low, mechanical wail. The deafening blast knocked the wind out of some of the Alliance troops near the gatehouse as they ducked shards of whistling shrapnel. The warplanes struck at least eight more times during the day, shattering buildings and shredding bodies. But surviving Taliban resurfaced after each attack and fought on fiercely until after nightfall, lighting the frigid blackness over Mazar-i-Sharif with red tracers. In the darkness, the coalition troops on the ground pulled back because they were unable to tell the Alliance Afghans from the Taliban. They rallied at the gatehouse around dusk and headed back to the area compound, only to return early the next day to find the battle still deadlocked.

Early on the second day of the uprising, the coalition troops called for bombing runs on the inner yard much more powerful than the ones unleashed the day before. Tragically, the first strike missed its target. The bomb tore into the fortress's northern wall, flipped a tank and scattered dead and wounded Alliance soldiers across the northern grounds. Those who could walk staggered from the clouds of dust with their eyes and ears bleeding as they cried for help. In the armory yard, the foreigners dug in further as the Americans and British spent most of the afternoon dealing with the accidental casualties.

As darkness fell on the second day, Qala-i-Jangi remained locked in a bloody struggle that seemed unthinkable given the massive forces arrayed against a paucity of combatants holding an area slightly smaller than a football field. Airstrikes, tank fire, and ground forces had failed to beat back the Taliban largely because they had become so heavily armed from the fort's weapons cache. The gun battle in the yard was playing out almost like urban warfare, a fighting style the al-Qaida–trained foreigners knew much better than the Alliance Afghans. Bin Laden's training camps had provided the Ansar with some of the best urban guerrilla warfare training available in the world. The Alliance Afghans, on the other hand, often didn't even aim when firing their guns. Moreover, the same ill discipline within the Alliance ranks that had allowed the prisoners to keep their arms also worked to prolong the battle. For every Northern Alliance solider fighting, perhaps five more idled outside the walls, infuriating the American and British forces on whom it fell to smash the resistance.

Nearing midnight on day two, an American AC-130 gunship rumbled through the darkness as it approached Qala-i-Jangi. In loping passes all night, the plane laid down a horrifying stream of cannon fire that sounded like a rain of jackhammers. One particularly well-targeted attack run shook the southwest quarter violently as the armory went up in a fireball that blew open doors ten miles away, scattering weapons and munitions all over the compound.

In the wake of that attack, the Ansar brigade began to show signs of withering, as the sun rose on day three of the revolt. One desperate prisoner had tried to escape the battle during the chaos of the night, but locals caught and lynched him not far from the fortress.

"We appreciated that," said Alliance Gen. Gul Ahmad. Ahmad and other commanders felt certain they had the upper hand at last. The gunfire had slowed, and the prisoners had no water and only rotting horsemeat for food. At around 10:00 A.M., Alliance forces inched into the Taliban area. They immediately faced several more suicide grenade attacks and sporadic fire that lasted until well after noon, when the fortress finally began to grow quiet.

Gradually, the few wounded fighters still above ground grew too weak to fight off Alliance troops, who moved in to find at least two bloody, gasping foreigners on the blackened earth. An Alliance solider finished one off with a spray from his Kalashnikov. Another Alliance troop decided to save a few bullets when he found a Talib struggling in a ditch; he brained him with rock. Eventually, only sounds from the smoldering armory broke the silence as Alliance soldiers began nervously picking through the hundreds of dead Taliban spread across the yard amid the bloated carcasses of dozens of horses. The fight seemed over.

Simon Brooks, a Red Cross official, went to the fort that Wednesday to head up the collection of the bodies, including Spann's. All was still as Brooks entered the inner yard and saw the aftermath of the battle.

"There was this tranquility, this macabre tranquility which pervaded the scene — dead horses, dead people, and these fir trees sort of cut off half way, completely shredded from the fighting and the bombing and this cold, it was very cold," recalled Brooks, a tall Australian with a mop of wavy hair and wide blue eyes. "The process of death obviously was extremely violent, and after death, this calm, this gruesome, silent sort of calm."

The ground was a carpet of scattered arms and ammunition thrown all over the area during the fighting, and Brooks moved gingerly through the yard.

"There was just this debris of unspent ammunition, rockets, mortar rounds, rifles, mortar tubes," Brooks said. "It was difficult to comprehend the quantities of ammunition — most of it live. Everywhere you walked you walked on this stuff."

The only thing stirring amid the scene was a single horse that had somehow miraculously survived, tethered in the middle of the grounds throughout the ordeal, though suffering an ultimately fatal leg injury. The horse's rear right hoof dangled from a twitching leg, nearly severed. Brooks saw the horse and asked one of Dostum's soldiers to shoot it and end its misery.

"He just turned to me and grinned," Brooks recalled of the soldier. "It was the only pathetic creature that had survived this whole thing and it was clearly suffering tremendously."

As Brooks and others culled the ruins for bodies, shots suddenly sounded from the cellar, shocking everyone who had been certain that all the prisoners were dead and the fight over. Alliance soldiers had ordered five local workers into the basement to search for bodies. As the group inched into the gloom, hold-outs guarding the entrance opened fire, killing one and injuring two.

By this time, Red Cross officials had collected about 240 bodies for burial at a communal site fifteen kilometers from the fort, leaving nearly half the 400 captives originally estimated unaccounted for. Clearly, a number remained in the basement, including Lindh, who had stayed in the cellar nursing his wounded leg throughout the fighting. The surviving workers who had gone down for the bodies had caught a glimpse of dozens of fighters on their feet, but no one would volunteer to take an official head count. The Alliance forces refused to negotiate with the remaining fighters after the carnage of the revolt, which by then had already left roughly one hundred Alliance soldiers dead and as many others wounded. So Gen. Faqir Mohammad ordered his men to kill them all.

Alliance soldiers gathered around the basement's tiny above-ground ventilation shafts and began tossing in grenades, chasing each throw with machine gun fire. They shot rocket-propelled grenades into the mouth of the basement's back entrance ramp. But even after several explosions lit the inside of the cellar, signs of life still leaked from the bunker, where Lindh and the remaining Taliban would hold out for several more days.

Inside, the rebels posted two guards at the entrance of the basement to fend off anyone who would dare enter. No one did after the body collectors were killed, but Alliance fighters continued to drop grenades into the basement through the air ducts and occasionally fired rockets down the ramp, shattering the concrete walls around the entranceway.

Bloodstains smeared the walls where the Taliban crouched in the fetid cellar with no food or water, occasionally sniping at Alliance forces from the mouth of the back ramp. Lindh and other holdouts took cover in the underground darkness, hunching over the bodies of their dead and wounded comrades, where at night temperatures neared freezing. Lindh was without his shoes, which had been taken by one of Dostum's men before the uprising. He fumbled barefoot, toes numbed by frostbite, over the packed rock and mud of a cellar floor littered with spent bullets and unwound turbans. The bullet in his thigh and the frostbite eating at his toes were but two of the pains he felt. He carried shrapnel wounds in his shoulder, ankle, and foot from the grenades tossed into the basement at random intervals.

Lindh had only eaten a small amount of food during his first two days in the cellar and had had just a few sips of water. After the food and water ran out, he had nothing to eat and grew weaker with each passing day. Lindh and the other prisoners felt certain Dostum's soldiers would kill them even if they gave up, and they talked a lot about the recent massacre at the Mazar-i-Sharif schoolhouse. Thus, despite their grave injuries, hunger, and thirst, the holdouts refused to surrender.

Outside, Alliance troops plotted new, creative ways to kill them. Frustrated and frightened, since the Ansar fighters remained defiant even four days after the main battle had ended, the Alliance troops poured fuel into the basement to torch those still underground.

The pungent liquid drenched Lindh as it gushed into the cellar through the vents, sending fuel-soaked prisoners scrambling into different rooms. Lindh, increasingly weak from his wounds, hunger and dehydration, crawled on all fours away from the vents as Alliance guards lit the fuel, sending flames coursing through the cellar. Lindh managed to avoid catching fire, despite the fuel on his clothes. Flames engulfed several other prisoners, who thrashed around as they burned alive, filling the basement with a heavy smoke and the stench of burning flesh. The fumes choked everyone, including Lindh, who passed out in one of the adjoining rooms. Meanwhile, the Alliance fighters poured fuel into and lit a fire in another area of the basement where the prisoners were huddled trying to avoid smoke and flames. Lindh awoke later as the smoke cleared with the taste of fuel heavy in his mouth. His surviving comrades began to stir as well, and above ground the Alliance fighters began shooting rocket-propelled grenades down the basement ramp again. Several prisoners had huddled at the bottom of the ramp to avoid the flames, only to be torn apart by the grenades, which littered the basement floor with bodies and dismembered limbs.

Firearms and fire having failed, on the sixth day of the prison revolt, Alliance fighters attempted to drown the remaining Taliban by redirecting an irrigation stream into the basement. Their endeavor flooded the hold with filthy, freezing water that became a waist-high, icy swamp of human excrement, blood, corpses, and body parts. The water decided many fates, as those too wounded to stand drowned, leaving roughly sixty mangled bodies floating through the cellar.

As the frigid water poured into the basement, Lindh struggled to his feet and propped himself between a stick and the shoulder of another soldier nearby. At one point, as Lindh fought to remain standing, he tripped over a corpse and plunged into the water

momentarily before hauling himself back up. Lindh spent approx-
imately twenty hours on his feet in the water as it slowly receded,
but not before he and others, desperate with thirst after days with
nothing to drink, had gulped mouthfuls.

As the water lowered, the smell of the dead thickened, filling
the basement with the choking stench of sodden, decaying
corpses. The wills of the last of the holdouts were broken. The
water had rendered the weapons the Ansar fighters held useless.
Starved and wounded, they chose to risk execution or torture by
Dostum's men above ground, rather than suffer further hell in the
cellar.

"The basement was too strong for RPGs," General Faqir said.
"We poured in gasoline and torched them, but that didn't get such
good results either. So we flooded them, and then they came up."

Faqir and other Alliance troops thought that perhaps a handful of fighters had survived. All were astonished when eighty-six
finally emerged in surrender, one day short of a week from the
revolt's first shots. Among the half-dead fighters who staggered
out at last was Lindh, who trudged from the basement and was
met at the top of the entrance by two Alliance guards. He had
been in the basement for about seven days and reeled with dizzi-
ness. Guards grabbed him under the arms on each side, bound
him tightly behind the back and walked him through the rubble
of shattered buildings and past the litter of bodies and unspent
munitions.

The guards led Lindh through the gates and shuffled him
toward some open metal storage containers off to the side where
the prisoners who had come out before him were laid out waiting
for food, water, and medical care. Lindh was seated with some
other prisoners in one of the containers, which quickly became
overcrowded with sick and dying men. As he sat on the metal
floor, the last of Lindh's strength began to leave him. Pain

wrenched his abdomen, where the filthy water he had ingested sloshed in his stomach, leaving him doubled over in agony. Eventually, Lindh and the other prisoners were loaded onto the bed of a truck, which was to take them to the prison in Sheberghan.

As Lindh curled up on the truck with the others, he noticed a crowd had gathered. He spotted some reporters, as well as an official from the Red Cross. Lindh asked the Red Cross official for help loosening his tight restraints, but the aid worker said he could do nothing since Dostum's men controlled the prisoners. Then a reporter began talking to him, telling him that Dostum's men had suffocated many of the Konduz captives in these storage containers. The reporter also said Lindh should consider himself fortunate to be in the presence of the media and the Red Cross, otherwise Dostum's men would likely execute them without hesitation. Soon the bed was full, and the truck lurched out of the compound, with Lindh and the dying wounded freezing in their wet clothes during the three-hour drive through the winter night to Sheberghan.

CHAPTER EIGHT

Fame, Fear, and a Passage Home

NICKNAMED "the Palace" by Dostum's men, the general's Sheberghan guesthouse sat in the middle of a decrepit warren of tumbledown concrete and mud houses clustered in ramshackle blocks like a third-world slum in search of a city. The Palace stood behind high walls about two stories above anything else in town. Hardly regal, the place could have doubled for a cheap Miami motel, with its two stucco buildings painted in pink and blue pastels. Creaky antennae and a battered satellite dish leaned from the roofs over an empty swimming pool surrounded by cracked blue tile and green turf pocked with cigarette burns.

Twelve Green Berets, two Air Force bomb guiders, and three CIA operatives, including Spann, had been traveling with Dostum since October, when they were assigned to help his faction of the Northern Alliance as part of the U.S. campaign in Afghanistan. Author Robert Young Pelton had joined Dostum's entourage during the uprising at Qala-i-Jangi, having arranged to take a small CNN crew with him on a month-long assignment profiling the warlord for *National Geographic Adventure* magazine. Pelton had quickly become friends with many of the Green Berets, who recognized Pelton's burly mug from his books and television appearances.

Pelton and the Green Berets were watching television at Dostum's compound the night of December 1, 2001, when they heard a loud bang at the Palace gates. The group went out to find Dostum's men unloading dozens of wounded from two trucks and lining the prisoners up in a cold haze of swirling dust aglow with headlights. "I'm like, 'holy fuck,'" said Pelton, who had asked Dostum's men to show him any prisoners taken from the basement so he could interview them. Dostum's men had obliged, bringing all eighty-six men from the basement to Pelton. Like others, Pelton had heard that perhaps a handful of men remained in the basement and was stunned to see so many survivors. Many of the prisoners were barely alive and wailed in pain as Dostum's men pulled them off the trucks while Pelton and the Green Berets looked on.

"I noticed that they were all pretty much Arabs, Uzbeks, and a couple Western-looking guys," Pelton said, remembering how a few among the prisoners spoke some English. "I didn't really want to talk to them too long because they were in so much pain. I mean there were people with shattered legs and huge chest wounds."

Pelton took some pictures while the Green Berets urged him to be careful and stay back. Initially Pelton didn't notice Lindh, and after several minutes of photographing the group, he urged Dostum's men to take them to the nearby hospital.

"There were bodies on top of bodies," Pelton said. "It was very, very freaky, and I thought, look, this is not appropriate, to sit there and interview these guys, asking them questions when they're fucking dying. It's just tacky."

At the hospital, Lindh was unable to stand and had to be carried by stretcher into the makeshift emergency ward, where he was placed on the floor with the other wounded from the basement, all of them near death. A thick stench from infected wounds and unwashed bodies matted with feces, urine, and blood hung everywhere in the frigid room as Lindh lay along with the others, barely conscious. Afghan doctors slowly tended the men around Lindh, but many seemed beyond help. One of Dostum's personal cameramen had gone to the hospital and was taping the scene, turning his camera on the wounded one by one as the doctors asked each individual his name and nationality. Lindh wearily said he was American when the doctor came to him. Stunned, the cameraman ran from the ward back to the Palace to tell Pelton.

Bill, a Green Beret medic, watched over Pelton's shoulder as Dostum's cameraman showed them footage of one of the prisoners on the floor in the hospital saying his name was "John."

"I'm thinking, huh, I wonder who this guy is," Pelton said. He asked Bill to grab his medical bag, and the CNN cameraman to get his gear, while the group quickly readied for a trip to the hospital. Two other Green Berets, including the team's captain, also tagged along to see who the guy in the video was. Before leaving, Pelton requested that the Green Berets restrain themselves until he figured out the guy's identity, worried that the soldiers might be confrontational when faced with a prisoner from the uprising in which their comrade, Spann, had been killed. They assured Pelton that they would not interfere and acted cool and professional at the hospital. There, Pelton, Bill, and the others saw firsthand what the Afghan cameraman had shown them. Lindh lay on the floor among the others, slipping in and out of consciousness, as an Afghan doctor stood over him, shouting questions, rapping his head whenever he trailed off while talking.

"What is your name?" the Afghan doctor yelled in heavily accented English at Lindh, who struggled to open his eyes as he faintly mouthed answers. "The American name, huh? Jones? The father's name? From? Where from?"

Lindh stammered something barely audible about being born in the U.S. capital and then closed his eyes.

"Washington, D.C.?" the doctor said. "Which part of Washington, D.C.? What part? Open your eyes."

"Northwest," Lindh said.

"What?" the doctor yelled, seeming to grow frustrated.

"Northwest," Lindh repeated.

"Northwest?" the doctor said again.

"Washington, D.C.," Pelton interrupted.

"Oh, oh, I see," the doctor said. "How many months ago you come to Afghanistan?"

"Can I ask him the questions?" Pelton said, brushing the doctor aside in the hope of stopping another crack to Lindh's head. "Hey, John. This is Robert Pelton, from CNN news. Where were you born? John?"

"United States," Lindh said. "Northwest."

"Huh?" the doctor blurted out again.

"Washington, D.C.," Lindh said.

"Washington, D.C.?" Pelton said. "Can you tell us if you have family in America?"

"All of my family is in America," Lindh said, speaking thickly as though his English was coming slowly back to him.

"And what is your mother's and father's name?" Pelton said.

"I don't know how that concerns CNN," Lindh said, waking up a little.

"I'm sorry," Pelton said. "We want to contact them to let them know you're still alive."

"CNN will contact them?"

"Yes," Pelton said. "We want to contact your parents to let them know you're still alive."

"I think I'd rather contact them through the Red Cross."

"Okay," Pelton said. "You want to talk to the Red Cross?"

"If I were to contact them I would contact them by a reliable source."

"So you want to speak to the Red Cross?"

"Later," Lindh said. "Tomorrow."

"Would you like an American trained medic to look at you?"

"If they are available."

"Yes, they're here right now," Pelton said. "Would you like them to look at you? They have a medical kit, and they can take care of your wounds."

"All right."

"Okay, are you injured?"

"Yes."

"What injuries do you have?"

"I have a bullet in my leg and several shrapnel wounds."

"Okay, well, they are here now," Pelton said. "They would like to attend to you. Do they have permission to take care of your wounds?"

"All right."

"All right, gentlemen," Pelton said, turning to Bill and the Afghan medics looking on. "Do you want to help him?"

The Green Berets stood back as Pelton arranged to have Lindh taken to a more private room. Pelton had met young men like Lindh before. A veteran adventure writer, Pelton had spent a lot of time in war zones, mostly traveling with jihadis. He had even met a few other American jihadis, so Lindh's presence, while surprising, did not come as a complete shock to Pelton. Most surprising to Pelton was Lindh's glib attitude and his initial refusal to accept any help. No Red Cross official was around to give Lindh a better option than Pelton's offer to relay a message home. And telling off Pelton, as Lindh initially seemed to do, would have meant remaining on the floor with dying men, waiting for care from Afghan doctors who appeared unconcerned about who lived through the night. What an idiot, Pelton thought, a typically self-righteous jihadi so wrapped up in his misguided religious convictions that he couldn't summon enough common sense to recognize the one person who might be able to help him get out of this mess. Pelton hadn't heard Lindh's story yet, though, and he wondered whether perhaps the boy was something besides a jihadi, maybe an aid worker caught up in the fighting. So he decided to question Lindh carefully without presumption and get as much on tape as possible.

Once in the separate room, Afghan medics removing Lindh's clothes felt a hard, round object, about the size of a grenade, in one of his pockets; everyone paused with dreadful anticipation. Pelton watched fearfully as the medics pulled the object from Lindh's pocket, remembering too clearly how many prisoners had blown themselves up in an effort to kill their enemies. The object turned out to be an innocent orange the Red Cross had given Lindh back in Mazar-i-Sharif. Pelton and the others sighed with deep relief as Bill set to work on him. From the look of his racked body, Bill immediately determined that Lindh suffered slight delirium and obvious dehydration and malnourishment.

"Can we shut the door?" Bill asked, hoping to stave off some of the winter cold and ease Lindh's hypothermia. "Make sure it's warm. Take off his sweater."

"John, is there some way we can contact your parents for you?" Pelton asked. "Do you have a number or some contact information?"

"Who are you?"

"I'm from the CNN news organization."

"All right," Lindh answered. "Look, you don't have permission to film me."

"Okay," Pelton said. "Well, that's not our concern right now. Our concern is for your welfare."

"All right," Lindh said. "If you're concerned about my welfare then don't film me and don't take pictures of me."

"Okay," Pelton said, leaving the cameras rolling. "Would you like some food, John? I brought some cookies."

"I haven't eaten in about more than a week."

"Would you like me to leave you some food as a gift?"

"I would appreciate."

"Okay, I will do that," Pelton said. "I'm taking your picture so that people can identify you and they can contact us because I think you need to let your family know that you survived."

"All right."

"All right," Pelton said. "Thank you, John."

"Thank you."

"You have nothing to say?" someone from behind the camera asked.

"You have to understand I have not eaten or slept in a long time," Lindh said. "I can't think very clearly right now."

"Is there anything you'd like to say that we can transmit and hopefully people will know that you're still alive?" Pelton asked.

"You mean to my family?"

"Yes. Just to let them know you're alive."

"I'll think about it," Lindh said. "Come back tomorrow and maybe we can put together a message or something."

"Okay," Pelton said. "Thank you. We'll see you tomorrow."

"Okay," Lindh said. "Thanks a lot."

"We'll let the doctors do their work," Pelton said.

"John," Bill said, meaning to ask Lindh about his wounds. But Lindh cut him off.

"My name is Abdul Hamid," Lindh said. "John was my name before."

"Okay, Abdul," Bill said.

"Abdul Hamid."

"Okay, Abdul Hamid," Bill said. "My name's Bill."

"All right."

"What is wrong?" Bill asked. "What happened?"

"I have a bullet in my leg, and I have shrapnel wounds," said Lindh, showing Bill the wounds along his back.

"Okay," Bill said. "How long ago was this?"

"Over the course of one week."

"One week from now, one week in the past?"

"Yeah," Lindh replied. "A week or eight days. The edge of a bullet hit my toe."

"Have you ever had an IV before?"

"Many times."

"Many times, really?" Bill said. "Since you've been fighting, you've had IVs many times?"

"No, since I was a kid."

"How old are you?"

"Twenty years old."

"Twenty years?"

"Yes."

"You're in good hands, I think you realize," Pelton said.

"Are you all right?" Bill asked Lindh. "You're hungry now, right?"

"Hungry and tired," Lindh said. "Several rockets, missiles and bombs exploding close to me."

"Can I ask how you ended up here?" Pelton asked Lindh.

"It's kind of a long story."

"I'd like to hear it," Pelton said.

"If you ask at a better time, I give you a better answer."

"I'll let you concentrate on what you're doing," Pelton said. "We saw you on videotape and we rushed down with these guys. You looked like you were in bad shape. There was a reporter here who shot a videotape of you."

"At the complex, at the military complex?" Lindh asked.

"No, you were on a stretcher I think and looked very close to being unhelpable," Pelton said. "So I got these men to come down and try to render some aid to you."

"This is an IV I'm giving you," Bill said, plugging Lindh's arm with a bagged cocktail that quickly sent badly needed fluids into Lindh's bloodstream.

"It has calories, so you don't have to eat," Bill added. "Okay, it will give you some energy. All right? It will replace some of the blood that you may have lost."

Then Bill said, "Abdul Hamid, do you speak Arabic?"

"I speak some Arabic," Lindh said. "I studied."

"Really?" Bill asked. "Where did you study Arabic at?"

"In Yemen."

"In Yemen?" Bill asked. "How did you end up in Yemen?"

"I had an interest in studying," Lindh said. "I knew some people from Yemen."

Bill and Lindh then began talking in Arabic, as the camera lights flickered and Pelton watched. When Lindh and Bill began talking in English again, Lindh was telling Bill where he was born.

"I couldn't tell you the name," Lindh said. "Columbia Women's Hospital."

"Columbia Women's Hospital?" Bill said.

"Northwest Washington, D.C."

"Northwest Washington, D.C.?" Bill said. "Alexandria? You've got an IV in you now. Okay? Let's see the rest of your wounds. You have a bullet wound in your leg?"

"They just put a dressing on it," Lindh said.

"The bullet is probably still inside," Bill said. "The bleeding is stopped so it's not really a big problem. Okay?"

"Okay."

"Your wounds don't seem to be very bad," Bill told Lindh, saying his biggest problem was malnourishment. "Just fighting is what's made you so tired and weak."

Pelton then began a detailed interview with Lindh, who became more alert as he warmed up and felt the effect of the calories in the fluids Bill gave him.

Lindh began to speak openly with Pelton as Bill continued to tend to his wounds. CNN's camera captured the exchange between Lindh and Pelton, an interview that would soon air to become one of the most memorable and shocking televised moments to come out of the war.

"When the gunshots started, everybody stood up and ran," Lindh said, recounting his experience during the opening moments of the uprising. "And I was—the whole time I was just up against the wall."

"And you came from Konduz?" Pelton asked

"All of us," Lindh said. "From Konduz, all of us were in Takhar."

"Takhar."

"The province."

"Yes, I know," Pelton said. "How long have you been in Afghanistan?"

"About six months."

"Why didn't you ask some Americans or foreigners to help you?"

"I was in Konduz. I didn't know any Americans."

"If you were a noncombatant, there were no outsiders?"

"In Konduz?"

"Yes."

"Really, at the time, I was unable to investigate that," Lindh said. "Well, actually when I came back—when we withdrew from Takhar, we walked by foot maybe more than a hundred miles. Afterward, I was very sick for the whole period. Until we came through Mazar-i-Sharif, I was still sick. So I wasn't really in a condition to be able to research."

"But were you with the Taliban all that time, or doing something else?"

"The Taliban have suffered much in the army, and they have the Afghans, and they have the non-Afghans," Lindh said. "I was with the separate branch of the non-Afghans."

"And what is the non-Afghani branch called?"

"It's called Ansar," Lindh said. "It means the helpers."

"Is that the same as the 055 brigade?"

"I'm not familiar with that."

"That's the term—I was with the Taliban in 1995, and they were explaining, they had the 055 brigade."

"It has—they have a number name," Lindh said. "I don't remember the number."

"Have you a slight accent?"

"I haven't spoken English with native speakers in several months. I've been speaking Arabic. I have been living overseas for about two years or so."

"Really, and how did you get to Afghanistan?" Pelton asked. "Because some friends of mine fought in Chechnya. Did you go through the Muj Trail, or did you just come here and volunteer?"

"I was a student in Pakistan studying Islam," Lindh said. "And I came into contact with many people who were connected with the Taliban. I lived in a region in the northwestern province—the people there in general have a great love for the Taliban, so I started to read some of the literature of the scholars and the history of the movement. And my heart became attached to them. I wanted to help them one way or another."

"Do you have any military skills?"

"No."

"Did you attend any of those camps where they train you?"

"A simple training camp."

"Because a friend of mine was American, and they had to hide him from the secret service all of the time, and he went to fight in Kashmir."

"In Pakistan, yes, that's how it is."

"After this is all done, how do you feel?" Pelton said. "You feel like you were sort of—you did the right thing? Well, do you feel now, after there's been a number of losses on the Taliban side . . ."

"With regard to this particular incident, you mean?"

"Yes."

"This was all a mistake of a handful of people."

"Could you explain that to me, because I'm very interested in that?"

"I'm sure you're familiar with the story," Lindh said, retelling how his group had ended up at Qala-i-Jangi after being halted outside Mazar-i-Sharif. "When they stopped us on the way and they said, 'Give all of the weapons,' many people were hesitant. So many of them held—they hid inside of their clothes hand grenades, which is against what we had agreed upon. And this is against Islam. It is considered a major sin to break a contract, if you agreed, especially with military situations. So some of them kept hand grenades with them, and when we arrived in the military complex in Mazar-i-Sharif, I think some of—I don't know what nationality or who they were exactly—but some of us, some of the brothers were very tense."

"This is going to feel a lot better," Bill said, adjusting the IV. "I'm giving you morphine now, okay? This is going to take away a lot of the pain."

"It's going to be happy juice," Pelton said.

"Happy juice?" Lindh said before going on. "As soon as I came down from the truck that we arrived in, a grenade exploded right next to the truck. Someone, I don't know what he was thinking or what he was doing—they blew up—a grenade. So the Dostum authorities became afraid of us, and they thought that maybe we had deceived them or something like this. So they immediately put us in the basement for the night, and I don't know if they intended after that to let us free or to interrogate us somewhat and then let us go or what they intended. So what happened was, we spent the night under the basement. Then they let us out one by one. They would search each one of us. Then they tied us up, and they put us out on the lawn. So, as they were taking us one by one, some of the last people to come out—again, they were, I don't know, they were afraid or whatever—they did the same thing. They pulled out a grenade, and they—anyway, somehow, they started fighting, starting with a grenade." Lindh added, "Eventually, they took some heavier weapons, and they took control of weapons in the storage house and some other things."

"You were there," Pelton said. "Did you run? Did you stay in the basement?"

"I was in the basement the whole time," Lindh said. "I didn't see anything that went on. I just heard the noise."

"The noise," Pelton said. "What made you decide to leave the basement?"

"It was the last day," Lindh said. "What happened was, yesterday, they had bombed us with airplanes. They had shot missiles. They had thrown grenades. They had shot us with all types of guns, poured gas on us and burned us. They had done everything you can imagine. So the last day they poured water in the basement. They wanted to fill it up with water. So when they filled it, most of us were injured at that point anyway. Actually, after the—maybe—first day, maybe about half of us or more than half were injured.

"So the last day, when they poured the water into the basement, I think the vast majority of us had drowned that morning—and we were standing in the water, the freezing water in the

basement for maybe twenty hours. And so after the water had receded somewhat, after the water receded somewhat, and you
know, we began to discuss with one another—just the topic was
on our minds, naturally, you know the basement was filled with
the stench of bodies, and we didn't have any more weapons. They
said, 'Look, we're going to die either way. If we surrender, then
they'll kill us.' Is it better to be killed—I mean, if we surrender,
the worst that can happen is that they'll torture us or kill us,
right? So right here in the basement, they're torturing us and killing us. So we might as well surrender, so at least we might have
a chance to—"

"Was your goal to be shahid, or martyred?"

"It's the goal of every Muslim."

"Was it your goal, though? Was it your goal at that time?"

"I tell you, to be honest, every single one of us, without any
exaggeration, every single one of us was one hundred percent
sure that we would all be shahid . . . all be martyred," Lindh said.
"But you know, Allah chooses to take a person's life when he
chooses. And we have no control."

"And there's a lot of talk on the news that bin Laden is behind
Ansar and things like that," Pelton said. "Is that your understanding?"

"No, he is not," Lindh said. "Ansar is composed of different
branches according to ethnic groups. It's because of management,
and of course, we all have the same cause, which has nothing to
do with ethnicity or anything like that. But the language is divided into Bengali and Pakistani and Arabic. So the Arab section
of the Ansar is funded by Osama bin Laden. Also the training
camps that the Arabs train in before they come to the front line
are all funded by Osama bin Laden."

"So when you are an American, how do you converse—you
were using Arabic to converse?"

"Yes, I studied Arabic."

"So would you be with the Arab fighters?"

"I was with them," Lindh said. "Actually, originally, I came with the Pakistanis, but they sent me to the Arabs because I don't understand Urdu."

"If you don't want us to, we won't," Pelton said. "But is there something that we can communicate? We have cell phones. Is there something we can communicate to someone, a loved one or a family member?"

"Would it be possible tomorrow? I'd like to give it some thought to actually what I'd say."

"So would you like us to come back tomorrow?" Pelton asked. "Just so you know, I'm not going to release your location when I talk about this. I'm not going to release your location, just for your peace of mind and your security. I'll come back tomorrow. And if you can think of anything you want us to contact either by Internet or by phone, or if you want to call yourself, I will bring a satellite phone."

"You have an Internet connection?"

"Yes, we do," Pelton replied. "So if you give us an e-mail address, we can send a message or we can bring the computer and you can type it."

"It is easier for me to write a message."

"So what I'll do is, I'll bring a laptop computer tomorrow," Pelton said. "And then we'll plug it in, and we'll go into whatever e-mail address you want."

"I would appreciate that."

"You know, first, I want to say that I've known very few Americans that have fought jihad," Pelton said. "And I'm just wondering, just personally, because I've been in jihad in Chechnya and southern Philippines, I'm just curious, was this what you thought it would be? Was this the right cause or the right place?"

"It is exactly what I thought it would be."

"Have you thought of fighting jihad in places like Chechnya?"

"Any Muslim that's concerned for the affairs of Muslims has considered this, I think."

"But you chose Afghanistan, and one thing that I always wondered was, you have Muslims fighting Muslims here."

"That's a question that's actually addressed in the Koran itself," Lindh said. "If there is an Islamic state—I mean there are certain situations in which Muslims, by necessity, are fought. For example, if a group of Muslims were renegades against the Islamic state."

"I'm an author of a book called *The World's Most Dangerous Places*, and I traveled with jihad groups through various places."

"Yourself a Muslim?"

"No, unfortunately, I'm not," Pelton said. "But I respect the cause and I respect the call, but I'm just interested to find an American, because when I met the other prisoners, who were in very bad shape, they seem to be from a number of very poor countries. You know, there were people from Yemen. There looked like one—have you met Chechens at all?"

"I've known a few Chechens."

"I've always wondered, because I've been searching for Chechens," Pelton said. "I've always wondered why a Chechen would fight here."

"Here, in Afghanistan, I haven't seen any Chechens," Lindh said. "Only some."

Pelton put just a few more questions to Lindh to confirm the legitimacy of his story, asking him mostly about the other soldiers he knew, in particularly a fighter named Abdul Aziz, the man believed to be the leader of the convoy from Konduz.

"Did you make friends?" Pelton asked.

"Of course, I made friends."

"And did you enjoy the jihad?" Pelton said. "I mean, was it a good cause for you?"

"Definitely."

"Is there something that I can broadcast?" Pelton said. "Something you would like to say to anybody? I don't think your wounds are life threatening."

"It's difficult for me to give you any interesting statement or anything at this point," Lindh said. "My mind is just exhausted."

"Just let the morphine take effect so you can relax," Pelton said. "Thank you for talking to us. By the way, I don't think you have to fear for your security."

"If you don't mind me asking, where are we exactly?" Lindh asked.

"This is Sheberghan," Pelton said. "They have an old Russian prison here that they are putting the jihadis in and also the regular Afghan Taliban. They are a little nervous because of the incident at Qala-i-Jangi, so what they're doing is they're trying to do the best they can for the prisoners. But there's quite a few and you'll probably get better treatment here in the hospital with the blankets and the heat and everything."

"I'm sure."

"So if you can, stay here," Pelton said. "I'm not going to tell anybody you're here so hopefully you can get some peace and quiet. But I will communicate anything you want to anybody."

"Thanks."

"This is Dostum's hometown. You picked a good place to be kept."

"How do you think his wounds are?" Pelton asked, turning to Bill.

"What we thought was a bullet wound we think is probably just a grenade wound, and the shrapnel is already come out," Bill said. "He is in a lot better shape than most of them."

"He said he lost a piece of his toe," Pelton said.

"The small of my back," Lindh interjected.

"We'll roll you over and take a look at your back, okay?" Bill said.

"I brought some cookies," Pelton said as Bill eyed the wounds on Lindh's back.

"I wouldn't worry about that," Bill told Lindh. "Are you an American citizen?"

"Yes."

"You're an American citizen, right?" Bill said.

"Yes."

"Well, right now you're a prisoner," Bill said.

"All right."

"Do you understand why?" Bill said.

"Of who?" Lindh asked. "A prisoner of the American government?"

"Do you understand why?" Bill asked Lindh again.

"Of who?" Lindh asked once more. "A prisoner of the Americans?"

"Dostum!" someone in the back of the room shouted.

"We should get him to Dostum's house," Bill said. "He can be moved tonight. There's nothing stopping him from being moved tonight as far as health-wise, other than the fact that he's weak. That's the biggest thing. He's been moved all the way up here in the back of a truck."

"He'll probably be asleep in about ten minutes," someone off-camera said.

"Yeah, what we gave him, he'll be out," Bill said. "We'll be carrying him. If we can put him over there in a room that we are watching."

"Yeah, we can move him there tonight," one of the other soldiers said.

"Upstairs, let's do that," another added.

"I don't think his wounds are—his wounds are not bad enough," Bill said. "He could walk off and never get any treatment and be fine. As long as he gets some food."

The Green Berets and Pelton carried Lindh from the hospital through the room filled with the uprising's survivors, most of whom were either already dead or in their last moments.

"So will most of these people be okay?" Pelton asked one of the hospital workers as they passed through the room.

"No," came the response.

☪

Back at the Palace, the Green Berets carried Lindh into the same building they were staying in and put him in an upstairs corner room. After some initial questioning, the Green Berets bid him a goodnight of sorts: they warned him that if he tried to escape Dostum's men would shoot him before he made it off the compound grounds. Too weak even to walk, much less make a dash for escape, Lindh spent the night in a deep, drugged slumber in a safe bed courtesy of Dostum. In the end, the warlord whose reputation Lindh had feared so much had saved his life and played a role in handing him back into American hands. As Lindh drowsed beneath a kitsch chandelier of crystal grapes, Pelton's interview began to air on CNN December 2 (and again on December 3 and December 19). Lindh's strange celebrity was born.

Lindh's instant fame meant little to the Green Berets, who woke him up early the next morning, bound his arms and blindfolded him. The troops told Lindh only that he was going on a long drive and that he should not talk during the trip. Sleet and snow fell from low clouds as Lindh, barefoot and dressed in flower-print pajamas, was helped into a truck at the Palace. The three-car convoy set out from Sheberghan to Mazar-i-Sharif, where he was taken to the main coalition base in the area, an unused high school built with aid funds from Turkey, referred to simply as the Turkish school. Unable to stand on his own, Lindh hung limply between two U.S. soldiers as they carried him into the drab, yellow school building and down a long hall to a ground-floor clinic, where he was laid out and looked over further by military medics.

Simon Brooks, the Red Cross official, had heard that the Americans had taken custody of Lindh and perhaps other detainees. Brooks went to the Turkish school with colleague Olivier Martin to request access to any war prisoners so he could register and interview them according to the Red Cross mandate.

"Even then we could understand the profundity of Lindh's position once it had become clear that he was here," Brooks said, describing how word of Lindh's presence in Mazar-i-Sharif had sent dozens of journalists scrambling to find him. "There was a hell of a lot of media attention."

American authorities at the base greeted Brooks and Martin professionally, acknowledged Lindh's presence in the school, led the two humanitarians to his bed in the clinic, and handed over a recently written dossier of his condition.

"He had obviously received a thorough examination and was receiving treatment for his wounds," Brooks said, adding that Lindh showed no signs of having been mistreated.

Martin and Brooks were unable to interview Lindh, however, because he was largely incoherent. He appeared heavily drugged and showed signs of mental trauma.

"We didn't want to stress him too much," said Brooks, who knew Lindh initially as John Walker from Pelton's report. "He seemed a little bit disoriented simply because I think he was obviously suffering, I would suggest, a degree of shock. You can imagine this man had spent a large part of the preceding week underground in a compound that had been heavily bombed in very cold conditions without food. I think he was in an understandable state of shock."

Brooks went back alone to interview Lindh the next day, December 3, and found him awake and alert, even engaging in a way that seemed to diffuse the gravity his unique case held. "The seriousness with which people, the authorities, were treating this was quite profound," Brooks said, describing the heavy guard and accompanying sense of tension that surrounded Lindh at the Turkish school.

"To go into the room where this personality who had captured the imagination of certainly Americans, if not the majority of people in the world," said Brooks. "I mean, here was the first person who people were sort of saying 'the first foreign Taliban.' So you walk into the room, as you can imagine, it's—it's quite a special moment to come face to face with this person. So you go in there with a sense of, I would say, apprehension."

Lindh seemed either immune or oblivious to the mood his presence set. "I think probably the thing that struck me most when I started talking to Walker was that he was almost disarming," Brooks said. "Here was a man who was extremely eloquent, who seemed actually quite in control."

Lindh had little to say, actually, other than that he had no complaints about the conditions of his detention. After some routine questions, Brooks asked Lindh if he wanted to send anyone a message, which the Red Cross could pass on to loved ones as part of its humanitarian mandate.

"Would you like to write a note to your parents?" Brooks asked.

"Yes, I would," said Lindh, who dictated a message Brooks scribbled onto a Red Cross form as a senior U.S. military officer looked on.

"Dear Mama and Papa," Lindh began as Brooks wrote.

"I apologize for not contacting you in such a long time. I realize this must have caused you a lot of grief. I am currently alive and well in Afghanistan and I am in safe hands. I cannot give you many details about my situation but it would be good to hear from you all."

Lindh signed "John Lindh" at the foot of the message, which Brooks passed through the Red Cross channels on to Lindh's family in California, where of course news of his capture was already in the headlines.

Brooks went back to the Turkish school some forty-eight hours later to check on Lindh again as part of the routine visits Red Cross officials conduct for prisoners of war. But Brooks was told Lindh was gone. Brooks assumed Lindh had been transferred, but in fact U.S. authorities had sequestered him for questioning nearby. The conditions about which Lindh had told Brooks he had no complaint became markedly less comfortable as military interrogators began questioning him in an effort to get battlefield information. They moved Lindh from the clinic to a room where a black cloth covered the only window, leaving him able to discern day from night only by looking for a glow along the edges of the drape. Armed guards stood over him at all times, and military interrogators visited him frequently.

Officials first questioned Lindh the same day he saw Brooks. Military personnel grilled him for about three hours, hoping to glean some insight into the murky world of the Taliban's and al-Qaida's ranks. Lindh's interrogators asked him about how the Taliban forces were organized, the botched surrender agreement between the Taliban leaders and Dostum, the uprising, and whether he knew anything about bin Laden's movements or plans for future al-Qaida attacks. They asked him to describe the camps he had been in and what sort of training he had received. They

asked him detailed questions about the nature of his combat instruction, quizzing him on what sort of soldier skills he had ac-
quired during his time with the Taliban. They also questioned him
about his travels in Yemen and Pakistan, and how he became involved with the Taliban. "Tell us everything," U.S. troops told
Lindh, even rumors.

The questioning lasted four days, during which Lindh offered
detailed and revealing answers that stunned his captors. Lindh
spoke in depth about his travels in Pakistan and Afghanistan, his
training days at al-Farooq, and his encounters with bin Laden.
He talked and talked, urged on by his interrogators who told him
that anything he knew might be able to save American lives.

Some of the soldiers who had to deal with Lindh grew dis-
gusted after learning where he had been and what he had done.
His guards in particular began to show open disdain, along with
traces of fear. They frequently called him "shit bag" and "terrorist," as well as "shithead," the latter being the nickname that
stuck. Lindh's guards warned him against trying to escape, despite his obvious weakness. One guard told him that they had him
"very surrounded," and he spent many hours blindfolded.

Between questioning sessions, Lindh was allowed to ask for
food, water, and bathroom visits, but when he asked for the time
so that he would know when to pray, his guards told him to "shut
up." Still, life in confinement proved far better than his days in
the basement. A medic visited Lindh every day in Mazar-i-Sharif,
keeping him dosed with antibiotics and painkillers. He greedily
ate the military ready-to-eat meals, wolfing down the packaged
peanut butter and crackers, granola bars, pasta, brownies, pears,
rice, spiced apples, and other goodies. They even came with a
moist towelette.

At some point during those initial days of questioning, which
lasted from December 2 to December 7, it struck Lindh that he

might need a lawyer, and he asked his military keepers when he could seek an attorney. The officers on hand neither had an answer for him nor seemed overly concerned with Lindh's request. They wanted battlefield information that might be of use to the ongoing conflict, not evidence of criminal wrongdoing. Orders had come from the Pentagon that Lindh was to be questioned about military, not criminal, matters. The FBI, U.S. officials decided, would ask any questions about possible law violations later.

On December 7, military officials planned to fly Lindh to Camp Rhino, the main U.S. base in Afghanistan outside Kandahar, not far from al-Farooq. In preparation for the journey, U.S. troops bound and blindfolded Lindh, tying his hands tightly together with plastic cuffs. On Lindh's blindfold U.S. troops scrawled "shithead," and they taunted him as they took turns posing for snapshots next to their infamous prisoner. One soldier told Lindh he was "going to hang" for his crimes and that upon his death the soldier would sell the souvenir "shithead" blindfold snapshots and give the money to a Christian charity. Another soldier told Lindh that he'd like to shoot him then and there. Instead, they marched him from his quarters, shoved him into the back of a van, and drove him to the Mazar-i-Sharif airport. There, they hustled Lindh onto a cargo plane.

On board, the plastic cuffs dug into Lindh's wrists, sending sharp pains through his arms. At some point during the flight Lindh began to beg the unseen troops around him to loosen the ties, screaming to be heard over the engine noise of the plane. Lindh's guards simply told him the cuffs weren't meant for comfort. And then Lindh began to grow scared.

"Please don't kill me," he pleaded, speaking blindly to the soldiers around him.

"Shut up," someone near said.

It was night when the plane touched down at Camp Rhino,

about seventy miles south of Kandahar. Lindh's guards initially put him face down on a stretcher, and he thought for a moment that he might be en route to his execution. The frigid winter air in the desert darkness swept cold over Lindh as the Marines unloaded him from the plane.

"Please don't kill me," Lindh begged again.

"Shut the fuck up," one of the Marines nearby said.

Lindh's guards cut off the clothes he had been given in Mazar-i-Sharif, leaving him naked as they bound him to a stretcher with duct tape wrapped tightly around his chest, upper arms, and ankles. Troops at Camp Rhino took more pictures of Lindh as he lay naked, taped to the stretcher, blindfolded in pain and fear. Then they placed him in yet another metal shipping container, where Marines questioned him for roughly forty-five minutes before leaving him to lie shivering, alone, crying. After some time, guards returned to wrap him in blankets, but left him bound so tightly that his forearms were pinned together in front of him pointing down. The Marines kept him like that for two days, inside his windowless compartment, not knowing when day passed into night. Small holes in the sides of the container provided the only source of air and light, through which troops yelled insults, swearing and loudly discussing how they planned to spit in his food. When Lindh needed to urinate, his guards simply propped up his stretcher vertically, leaving him bound.

Lindh began December 9 cold and hungry. He was given a meal with pork, which he refused to eat. His guards then gave him another meal and a new blanket. Shortly thereafter, Marine guards entered Lindh's container, tore off the duct tape, dressed him in a hospital gown and shackles, and then carried him on his stretcher, still blindfolded, to a nearby tent. When guards removed the blindfold, Lindh sat facing FBI Agent Christopher Reimann, who introduced himself and then immediately read Lindh his rights. When Reimann came to the point related to

one's right to an attorney, he said, "Of course, there are no lawyers here."

Lindh asked when he could see an attorney, but Reimann
only told him again that there were no lawyers available for him
in southern Afghanistan. Lindh then agreed to forgo his rights,
both verbally and by signing a written waiver form, and submit
to FBI questioning, despite assurances from Reimann that no interrogation would take place if Lindh insisted on the presence of
an attorney. Lindh feared that any refusal to cooperate with interrogations would mean crueler conditions of incarceration. He still
wore restraints as he signed the Miranda waiver.

Reimann questioned Lindh in three lengthy interrogation sessions over the course of two days. Lindh told him everything,
starting with his upbringing and earliest interests in Islam, to his
last days with the Taliban and how Pelton found him. He told
Reimann that he felt certain he would be prosecuted in the United
States, feelings he had expressed to his Harkat ul Mujaheddin
comrades on the eve of his journey to Afghanistan. Conditions improved for Lindh as he cooperated with Reimann. He was allowed to wear clothes and was no longer taped to furniture inside
his box, but Reimann's interrogations were shaping up as something bad for Lindh nonetheless. After his interviews with Lindh,
Reimann wrote a report nine single-spaced pages long, which
would soon become the cornerstone of the U.S. government's
criminal charges.

On December 14, a helicopter flew Lindh from Camp Rhino
to the U.S.S. *Peleliu,* a warship afloat about fifteen miles off the
coast of Pakistan, where he would remain for seventeen days.
When Lindh arrived aboard the *Peleliu,* he was too weak to walk
and had to be rolled around in a wheelchair. In surgery, the ship's
doctors removed the bullet from his leg and left him to recover in
the brig. His guards, handlers, and caretakers regarded him with
a mixture of fear, hatred, and dark curiosity.

By this time the persona shaped by the media coverage of his story loomed huge in the United States—and at sea aboard the U.S. warship. At least twice during Lindh's time on the ship, military personnel took souvenir photos with him, but officers ordered the pictures destroyed when they were discovered. Official pictures were taken as well to document his military jailing. In all, some three hundred photographs were taken of Lindh while he was aboard the *Peleliu*. As if he were a one-man freak show, military personnel snapped shots of Lindh while he was getting a haircut, receiving medical treatment, being transported, or just sitting in his room. But overall, things were improving for Lindh. When he didn't like the first haircut he got and asked for another, the ship's barber indulged him. He was allowed to talk to the four other captured Taliban fighters, including twenty-six-year-old Australian David Hicks. Their guards told Lindh and the others what time of day it was so they could offer their five prayers at the proper time. And the brig supervisor would call up to the deck to ascertain the direction of Mecca, so Lindh and his comrades would know which way to face when praying. They were also given Korans and allowed to shower twice a week.

When Lindh inquired about what might happen to him, his captors told him that his case was being discussed in Washington, D.C., and that a decision would come soon. In fact, President Bush himself had taken up the question with Secretary of Defense Donald Rumsfeld and Attorney General John Ashcroft. Bush even mentioned Lindh publicly on December 21 during a session with reporters in the Oval Office, where he was showing off a new rug.

"I've tasked the National Security Council to—to work up a strategy on how to deal with each and every person that we capture," Bush said when asked about Lindh, who was then still known most widely as John Walker. "And obviously Walker is unique in that he's the first American al-Qaida fighter that we have captured. And we will announce to the country when we have made up our mind on all—on how to deal with the wide variety of cases. Walker, himself, is being well treated on a ship of ours. He is—I suspect he's finding his berth a little better than it was when he was placed in the prison in Afghanistan. And, you know, we've heard—the administration has heard from his lawyer, and we've told his lawyer that at the appropriate time we will let everybody know, including his family, how we're going to proceed with Walker, as well as others that have become captured during this war."

On December 31, Lindh was moved to the U.S.S. *Bataan*, where he would remain for twenty-three days. By January 15, 2002, the government had filed an affidavit and obtained an arrest warrant for him, clearing the way for a civilian trial in the United States. Lindh left the *Bataan* on January 22, flying by helicopter to a military base in Pakistan, where he spent roughly three days handcuffed and blindfolded with a wrap that covered most of his face, sitting on the ground in a barbwire pen. Eventually, he was put on a C-17 military transport plane heading back to the United States.

Lindh's flight arrived at Dulles International Airport outside Washington, D.C., on January 23 at about six in the evening. Off the plane, military guards whisked Lindh to a waiting helicopter, which flew him to the nearby Alexandria Detention Center. A large group of heavily armed FBI agents watched as the chopper settled on a patch of lawn circled by police cars. A well-guarded Lindh shuffled slowly from the helicopter to a waiting van, which drove him through the jail's back entrance. After twenty-two months overseas, Lindh was again on native soil, arriving near the place of his birth in a changed country. An infamous and abhorred figure, Lindh faced criminal charges that could possibly mean a life in prison.

CHAPTER NINE

The Mercies of an Anguished Nation

FRANK LINDH had broken into sobs and nearly collapsed when he first saw the television images of his dazed son telling Pelton calmly how he had expected to die in Afghanistan. The following day, after regaining his composure, he called one of the best trial lawyers in San Francisco, James Brosnahan, and left him a voice mail. "I think my son has got a problem, and I'm wondering if you would represent him," Frank's message said.

It was a Sunday, so Brosnahan got the message while at home and called Frank Lindh back, telling him to come by his office in downtown San Francisco Monday to talk about the case. "I don't know if I'm going to do this," Brosnahan told Frank Lindh over the phone. "But maybe I will."

Brosnahan had seen Lindh on television the night before, too, and, for typical reasons, had concerns about representing someone who openly acknowledged joining the Taliban. Even so, Brosnahan quickly agreed to take the case after meeting with Lindh's parents and discussing things with a number of partners at his law firm, Morrison and Foerster. The first thing for Brosnahan to do, of course, was to talk to his new client. However, after his television debut, Lindh suddenly disappeared, remaining incommunicado in military custody, despite great efforts by his family and Brosnahan to reach him.

By December 4, Lindh's parents had tried to send a letter to him through the Red Cross. In the short note, Lindh's father told his son:

> Mama and I love you very much and are trying to find out where you are being held. I have retained a lawyer to help you. Please ask the US authorities to allow me and mama and the lawyer to come visit you as soon as possible. I hope you're feeling OK.

He signed the note "Papa" and wrote a postscript at the top saying that Naomi and Connell "both send their love!"

The senior Lindh wrote a similar note December 18, after getting his son's original Red Cross message "dated December 3—my birthday. You have our unconditional love and complete support. We are begging to get to see you. Trust in God!" He added at the bottom: "P.S. We hired a lawyer who also wants to see you!"

In a third letter dated December 27, Lindh's father told his son that he hoped to see him soon and that his attorney, "Jim Brosnahan, also wants to visit you with us. You will like him. We hope you are well. God bless you!" Lindh's mother assured her son about Brosnahan in a note of her own sent to the *Bataan* by an address the Defense Department gave to Brosnahan on January 3. Marilyn Walker wrote how she had prayed desperately in the months Lindh went missing.

> Finding you alive is the answer to all those prayers. You've been through so much! I just want to see you and hold you, hear your voice . . . Family and friends have been sending love and prayers your way as well. James Brosnahan is the attorney we have retained

to represent you and has already been at work on your case. He is a very good man, John, of great integrity, knowledge, and wisdom. He will be contacting you as well.

Lindh's parents, Brosnahan, and two other defense attorneys, Tony West and George Harris, were waiting in Alexandria for Lindh to arrive after hearing just days before of the government's plans to transfer Lindh for federal prosecution. They watched television coverage of Lindh's arrival from their hotels near the Alexandria Detention Center, where a crush of satellite trucks and media vehicles thronged the road when they drove to see him that evening. Jail officials told the family and attorneys that Lindh could see no one until the next morning, however, when he was scheduled to appear in federal court.

On the morning of January 24, 2002, snipers prowled the rooftop of the federal courthouse in Alexandria, looking over the horde of demonstrators, onlookers, and media. Frank and Marilyn arrived early with the lawyers before the morning hearing and were shown to the courthouse lockup. There, Lindh stood behind wire mesh in a green prison jumpsuit with "prisoner" stenciled across the back, his long hair cut and his beard shaved. Each parent took turns holding their hands against the mesh, with Lindh doing the same from the other side, the closest contact the parents could hope to have with their son. Twenty minutes later, they walked from the lockup crying. Marilyn hugged each of the attorneys tightly before they went in to meet their client for the first time. None of the lawyers knew quite what to expect from Lindh. Brosnahan had wondered if Lindh might show the same angry defiance displayed by other Muslims who had been taken into U.S. custody in connection with September 11, such as Zacarias Moussaoui. Brosnahan had told Frank and Marilyn on their way to the jail, "If we get there and, you know, he's all tied up in some crazy Islamic fundamentalist desire for a show trial or a political trial or something like that, I'm not going to be able to represent him."

Lindh appeared calm and composed as the lawyers entered the holding cell and sized him up from the other side of the wire mesh. "Boy, am I glad to see you guys," Lindh said upon seeing the team of attorneys his parents had brought for him. "I've been waiting to see you guys for a long time."

Everyone laughed, despite the gravity of the moment. "It was just so clear in that first meeting that we were dealing with such a sincere young man, who clearly had gotten himself into quite a mess," said West, the youngest attorney on the team, who wound up spending much of his time with Lindh in the months that followed. "He was not the demon that everyone from the Attorney General on down was saying he was."

Lindh spent about fifteen minutes with his lawyers, who immediately set to gathering details about the case and telling Lindh what to expect in the courtroom that day and in the weeks to come. Shortly thereafter, Lindh walked into a packed courtroom; his parents watched him from the second row. He sat alongside his attorneys before U.S. Magistrate Judge W. Curtis Sewell, who called Lindh to the podium for a reading of the criminal complaint the government had recently filed against him. Lindh stood silently as the judge outlined the charges, telling him he was accused of conspiring to kill fellow Americans, providing support to the terrorist groups Harkat ul Mujaheddin and al-Qaida, and aiding the Taliban. When asked if he understood the charges, Lindh said simply, "Yes, I do, sir." He also said he understood that the charges against him could lead to life in prison.

That largely ceremonial first hearing lasted only about fifteen minutes. The government's real case against Lindh began February 5, 2002, when U.S. Attorney General John Ashcroft unveiled a ten-count indictment against Lindh at a Justice Department news conference. "John Walker Lindh chose to train with al-Qaida, chose to fight with the Taliban, chose to be led by Osama bin Laden," Ashcroft told reporters. "The reasons for his choices may never be fully known to us, but the fact of these choices is clear."

Ashcroft's statements sounded bold and sure, but the indictment itself showed a government case that looked uncertain in some respects. For example, the government did not charge Lindh with treason, defined as aiding an enemy in a time of war and punishable by death. To convict for treason, prosecutors must either have a confession or two witnesses to any treasonous acts. Ashcroft's attorneys had neither. Instead, they had detailed statements by Lindh about his alleged crimes, offenses that had virtually no history of prosecution in the United States. Indeed, a case like Lindh's had never come before a U.S. court. And for all Ashcroft's indignation, the formal charges sounded like a reach, an overlapping collection of alleged offenses mostly related to sanctions, not terrorism, treason, or murder.

Specifically, the grand jury's indictment counts included conspiracy to murder U.S. nationals, conspiracy to provide material support and resources to Harkat ul Mujaheddin; providing material support and resources to Harkat ul Mujaheddin; conspiracy to provide material support and resources to al-Qaida; providing material support and resources to al-Qaida; conspiracy to contribute services to al-Qaida; contributing services to al-Qaida; conspiracy to supply services to the Taliban; supplying services to the Taliban; and using, carrying, and possessing firearms and destructive devices during crimes of violence.

If the prosecution's case had some weaknesses, however, one thing was clear: the government was bent on putting Lindh in jail for many years. A conviction on all counts in the indictment

would leave Lindh in prison for the rest of his life. Even a conviction on one of the lesser counts would add up to forty years in jail
because of the charge relating to the use of firearms and explosives. There seemed little way for Lindh to avoid prison, especially in the political climate created by September 11. Lindh was
set to go on trial on the anniversary of the attacks at a courthouse
less than nine miles from the Pentagon. The idea of a jury letting
him walk free seemed impossible, regardless of the legal complex-
ities of the case. Even Lindh's lawyers, his closest legal allies,
found some of what he told them of his time in Afghanistan extremely troubling. "Nobody likes the fact that he met Osama bin
Laden," West said. "No one was happy that he was at that camp.
Even though he wasn't training to be a terrorist, he was at a camp
that none of us would want our kids to be at."

Lindh had begun to understand the extent of the hatred and
anger focused on him while aboard the U.S.S. *Bataan.* He and
Australian Talib David Hicks had discussed how Lindh would
likely become a scapegoat. Lindh was the only high-profile captive the U.S. government had from Afghanistan. Taliban leader
Mullah Mohammed Omar remained missing, as did bin Laden
and most of the senior leadership of al-Qaida. Moreover, in the
United States, the anthrax killer (or killers) remained at large,
terrorizing an entire nation with its own mail. American popular
sentiment teemed with frustration, confusion, grief, fear, and rage
as Lindh arrived and drew abundant media focus with his court
proceedings.

"He understood the extremely difficult situation he was in,"
said Harris, who along with West and Brosnahan began spending
long hours with their client at the Alexandria Detention Center.
Lindh met with his attorneys for days on end in a small jailhouse
meeting room, where he sat with shackles on his hands and feet
at a round table across from the attorneys. "When he came back

to the United States, he fully expected that he was going to face pretty severe circumstances and very likely could spend a very long time in prison."

That sense deepened as Lindh began to learn more about the Taliban, bin Laden, and what had really happened on September 11. Lindh had heard only snippets of news since he crossed the border into Afghanistan. He had never even seen pictures of the September 11 terrorist attacks until West brought a laptop to the jail and played newscasts from that day for him. Lindh was shocked. "When he saw these moving pictures of these planes flying into buildings there was a guttural reaction," West said. "We all had it when we saw it, but he had it too."

To hear about the attacks is one thing. To watch them is another. Finally, Lindh began to truly grasp the enormity of what had happened and why he had become the focal point for so much animosity. "He could really understand why people were in the emotional state that they were in when he was found," West said.

Lindh heard still more disturbing news from his lawyers, who brought him articles and reports by human rights groups detailing the atrocities of the Taliban and the group's connection to al-Qaida. Prior to this personal enlightenment, Lindh believed he had been performing an obligation in line with his religious beliefs. In his mind, the Taliban were worthy Muslims fighting to establish the supreme law of Allah in Afghanistan, an admirable cause in the eyes of a certain brand of radical Muslims, among whom Lindh had spent much of his time for more than a year prior to his arrest.

"There were a lot of things that he didn't know," Harris said. "His own experience in Afghanistan was really quite limited; it was being a military trainee and a soldier on the front lines. So there was a lot about the Taliban government and society that he really didn't know."

These revelations came gradually to Lindh as he sat in isolation in his cell between meetings with his legal team. The things his lawyers explained left Lindh feeling guilty for his loyalty to the Taliban. He eventually came to a resigned understanding of why he was to be punished, given what had happened on September 11. He never complained to his attorneys about his situation or wondered aloud why fate had left him to pay such a heavy price for his mistakes. Instead, Lindh accepted the consequences he faced with a measure of objectivity. "He never said what most defendants say, which is 'why me?'" Brosnahan said. "He feels like he really made some mistakes . . . and he was wrong about some things."

Nonetheless, Brosnahan and the other defense attorneys tried to better their odds at trial in a series of hearings that went badly in legal terms for Lindh and underscored the difficulty of his situation. Brosnahan's efforts to get Lindh free on bail, have the government's charges dropped, and move the trial all failed. Through the spring of 2002, Lindh sat in court watching Brosnahan trade barbs with the presiding judge, who clearly grew angry with Brosnahan at times and obviously had little sympathy for Lindh. By June, the court had ruled against Lindh in seven motions filed by his attorneys. The court looked set to rule against Lindh yet again at a July 15 hearing meant to argue the admissibility of Lindh's statements to CNN and federal investigators, statements Brosnahan argued were coerced. Things looked increasingly bad for Lindh.

The prosecution team, led by U.S. Attorney Paul J. McNulty, was concerned nonetheless. Tentative talks about a possible plea deal emerged in June, with each side signaling initial offers through informal channels. Lindh heard about the prospect of a plea bargain then, but the talks seemed to stall in the following weeks as both sides prepared for crucial hearings.

Unbeknownst to Lindh and his lawyers, the prosecution was unilaterally preparing an offer to put on the table before the hearing on the admissibility of Lindh's statements. McNulty viewed that day, July 15, as an unofficial deadline, because, despite signs to the contrary, he feared the judge might suppress Lindh's statements, the core of the prosecution's case.

Even if the judge did not suppress Lindh's self-incriminating statements, McNulty felt that it would be in the government's interest to negotiate a plea agreement with Lindh. McNulty felt the government's case on count one, conspiracy to kill Americans, was actually the weakest point in the indictment. To convict on that count, McNulty would have to prove to a jury that Lindh's actions added up to some kind of participation in the September 11 attacks, a difficult legal argument. Moreover, the physical effort of assembling the case overall would be daunting.

The evidence and witnesses likely to be needed at trial were scattered all over the world. Some thirty U.S. servicemen would likely have to take part in the court proceedings, and many of them were still deployed in faraway locales. Lindh and his attorneys were pressing for access to detainees in Guantanamo Bay, Cuba, where military officials were loath to interrupt their ongoing interrogations for a trial. Despite ruling routinely against the defense, the judge had left open the possibility of allowing Lindh's defense team to call prisoners from Guantanamo Bay to testify, a ruling that could have potentially blown the prosecution's case. If the judge ruled in favor of the defense on the Guantanamo Bay witnesses, the government would be forced to either produce the prisoners or drop the charges. And it seemed unlikely that the military would escort newly captured detainees in the war on terrorism to Alexandria for Lindh's trial.

That was McNulty's chief concern, but there were others. People who had so far not surfaced in the media as part of Lindh's case would have to be present at trial. However, revealing their identities could possibly put them at risk of reprisals by either Islamic militants or enraged Americans of the kind who sent a steady stream of hate mail to Lindh, his family, and his attorneys. McNulty didn't want to begin that process if the case would eventually be settled out of court. So he began discussing the possibility of negotiating a plea deal through a chain of higher-ups that led all the way to the White House.

At the Justice Department, Ashcroft and others were open to the idea of a plea bargain, but wanted to ensure Lindh would get as much prison time as possible—requiring at least twenty years. At the Pentagon, Secretary of Defense Donald Rumsfeld demanded, as a condition of any deal, that Lindh retract his allegations of mistreatment at the hands of the U.S. military. Given that, Rumsfeld would have no objections, clearing the way for a final okay from the White House. On July 11, a Thursday, White House Counsel Alberto R. Gonzalez discussed the emerging deal with President Bush, who approved.

The next day, after another hearing at the courthouse, the prosecuting attorneys approached Lindh's lawyers and proposed that they meet to discuss a plea deal. Later that day, in McNulty's office, government prosecutors outlined the agreement to Lindh's lawyers, who later relayed it to Lindh in a somber conversation back at the jailhouse.

Lindh sat with Brosnahan, West, and Harris in the plastic chairs at the round table and listened as they explained the deal. They informed him that the federal system did not offer parole, but Lindh could potentially shave three years off of his sentence by accruing good behavior. Barring a pardon, he would serve seventeen years in a federal penitentiary. That was the best his future held. At a time when many boys his age were deliberating options for life after college, Lindh had the opportunity to choose between jail or, possibly, more jail. If the case went to trial, Lindh would most likely be convicted on at least one of the ten counts in his indictment, meaning he would face a sentence of forty years or more. Considering the risks of a trial, striking a deal clearly presented the better option. Still, seventeen years was difficult to accept. At age twenty-one, the time Lindh was to serve spanned roughly the length of his living memory. By the time Lindh walked free, Brosnahan, the oldest at the table, would likely be dead. Harris would be about Brosnahan's age, and West, the youngest attorney, would be close to Harris's age. In heavy silence, Lindh thought for a moment about the years—then cracked a smile.

"Wow," Lindh said. "That means I'll be as old as Tony when I get out." Again, they all laughed, breaking the sobriety of the moment. "It was typical John," West said. "We had just laid on this kid that he's going to spend the next two decades of his life in prison, and, you know, he defused the moment by making a little joke—at my expense, but a joke nonetheless."

Trying to give Lindh some hope, West showed him that he had no gray hairs. Harris couldn't match that claim, but told Lindh how his youngest child had been born when he was forty years old. With this, Lindh began to realize that he still could have a life ahead of him, which led him to make some demands of his own. Lindh adamantly refused to sign any agreement that carried convictions on counts that labeled him a terrorist. He continued to believe that his service with the Taliban had nothing to do with terrorism. Lindh also wanted to serve his time in a prison closer to his family, and he insisted on assurances that he could pursue an education while in jail. Further, any deal had to allow him to travel abroad upon his release, so he could make the obligatory Muslim pilgrimage to Mecca.

Brosnahan, Harris, and West left Lindh and got in touch with the prosecutor's office, opening a series of negotiations that lasted through the weekend. Ironing out details, attorneys from both sides went back and forth with phone calls and faxes until about one in the morning of Monday, July 15, when Lindh signed the final version, penning "John Lindh" at the foot of the document. The deal called for Lindh to plead guilty to aiding the Taliban, which was not officially a terrorist organization, and carrying a rifle and grenade while doing so, offenses that added up to twenty years. "We were getting a reasonable sentence that struck us as being a just resolution of the case," McNulty said.

Lindh's insistence that he did not join in terrorist activities meant nothing to McNulty and others in the government. Technically, the Taliban was the unrecognized government of Afghanistan, and not a terrorist organization. However, with an executive order issued in June of 1999, former President Bill Clinton had made any dealings with the Taliban by Americans illegal, citing the Taliban's support of bin Laden. Harkat ul Mujaheddin and al-Qaida, by contrast, both appeared on the State Department's list of foreign terrorist organizations. Lindh wanted to distance himself from those groups, which in his mind were distinctly different organizations with separate missions and aims—despite how interwoven all three were in reality. In the Justice Department's eyes, however, the Taliban, al-Qaida, and Harkat ul Mujaheddin represented the same criminal lot, violent men with violent aims, supporters and purveyors of terrorism, if not exactly defined as such in the strictest legal terms.

"In our mind, we thought that the distinction between the Taliban and [Harkat ul Mujaheddin] and al-Qaida was splitting hairs," McNulty said. "And we felt like in good faith we could represent to the court that this guy essentially engaged in conduct that involved on the one hand association with bad guys of one kind or another, and, two, taking up arms in the furtherance of that association."

As part of the deal, Lindh had also agreed to sit for further U.S. interrogations and aid in whatever way he could ongoing and future terrorism investigations, another incentive that made the agreement appealing to McNulty's office. Lindh had only ever been a lowly foot soldier in the Taliban, but he had nonetheless penetrated a world that the U.S. government, with all its intelligence resources, was still struggling to understand.

In the courtroom after signing the deal, Lindh rose before T. S. Ellis III, the federal district judge who had overseen the proceedings. Ellis asked Lindh a series of stock questions as the young man stood at the podium in his jumpsuit, his lanky frame slightly stooped, stating for the formal record his age, background, and intent to plead guilty.

"I provided my services as a soldier to the Taliban last year, from about August to November. In the course of doing so, I carried a rifle and two grenades," Lindh told the judge, as surprised reporters in the back row of the courtroom scribbled furiously into notepads and rushed out to make calls. "And I did so knowingly and willingly, knowing that it was illegal."

After the scheduling of his sentencing hearing, Lindh returned to the Alexandria jail and began a battery of government debriefings, sitting at times for hours with officials from a host of different government agencies. Lindh's attorneys, meanwhile, worked to ensure that Lindh could undertake distance-learning programs and, eventually, transfer to a prison closer to his family.

West told Lindh to view the time he would serve as a sort of intellectual leave. "You know, this is going to be a long sabbatical for you," West said to Lindh in one of their sessions that summer. "You'll get your college degree, and you'll be able to get a Ph.D. by the time you're out."

"I better get three Ph.D.s," Lindh said, smiling. "If I don't get at least three Ph.D.s, I'll be ashamed of myself."

All was not entirely settled, though. The judge still had to formally approve and impose the sentence, and Lindh would have to appear again in court, where he would be expected to speak.

"He's very shy and he doesn't like to speak in public," West said, describing how Lindh discussed the idea of giving a statement in court. "He knew how important it was for him to try to articulate to the best of his ability why he did what he did and his state of mind when he went to Afghanistan and what was motivating him. It was important for him to be able to say that in the most straightforward way that he could, and so he spent a lot of time writing and bouncing ideas off of us."

☪

Judge Ellis had scheduled Lindh's sentencing hearing for the afternoon of October 4, 2002, setting aside most of the day for proceedings he expected to go long. It was to be Lindh's last appearance in a public forum before disappearing for the better part of two decades. The usual media throng gathered outside the courthouse, where antennae from television vans rose like stripped flagpoles over a crowd of photographers, reporters, and cameramen waiting at the front steps for a glimpse of the lawyers or the Lindh family.

Lindh arrived at the courthouse through the back entrance, like always, and waited in the first-floor lockup, where Brosnahan, Harris, and West met with him just before he walked into court. Lindh had written and rewritten the statement he planned to give, drafting and revising, trying to come up with the right words. Lindh wanted people to understand that one could go to Afghanistan on jihad without being a terrorist. He wanted to explain somehow that people of the same religion fighting for the same cause in Afghanistan can be, nonetheless, many worlds apart, especially when it comes to acts like the September 11 attacks. Some of the men Lindh met at al-Farooq undoubtedly had a hand in planning the attacks, which Lindh and many of his former comrades had believed to be sacrilegious, as well as horrifying. Yet everyone at al-Farooq, from bin Laden down to Lindh, united in support of the Taliban, a cause Lindh only too late learned to be unjust.

Lindh read West, Harris, and Brosnahan a final version of his statement, tearing up a little as he went through it. The lawyers all reassured Lindh about his writing and coached him to read slowly, so that everyone in the courtroom would hear and understand. "This was the first time John was being given an opportunity to speak in all these months," West said. "The first time that the American people would hear his voice, and he had a lot to say."

Lindh's parents, brother, and sister sat near the front, ahead of rows crammed with reporters and other spectators, including Johnny Spann, the father of the CIA operative killed at Qala-i-Jangi. Spann's family had followed Lindh's court proceedings closely, believing firmly that Lindh bore some blame in the younger Spann's death, despite the government's admitted lack of evidence supporting the theory. Lindh's plea bargain outraged the Spann family, and the grieving father wanted to speak at the hearing before Lindh's sentencing. Judge Ellis knew Lindh's sentence would leave many unhappy, especially the Spann family, as he opened the hearing by going through the facts of Lindh's case at length, as required by the plea agreement. After laying out the details, Ellis continued with his own thoughts about the settlement.

"On the whole, it was a fair and just and reasonable resolution, maybe not the best," Ellis said. "But the most important thing to me was that the government did not have evidence that linked this defendant to the murder of Mr. Spann. Had I had that evidence, I would not have accepted the plea."

The judge did point to obvious questions that the plea deal left open, like Lindh's claims of ignorance about the nature of his al-Farooq trainers, even after they asked if he was interested in terrorist attacks on the United States or Israel. Lindh's assertion that he did not know of America's support of the Northern Alliance after September 11 also bothered the judge.

"I wonder whether he could not have deduced that those aircraft were a little too sophisticated for the Northern Alliance or the Taliban," Ellis concluded, turning finally to Lindh. "This is now your opportunity to say anything at all you wish. You have no obligation to address the court. You don't need to, if you don't wish to. But I hope you will take advantage of the opportunity."

"All right, I understand, sir," Lindh said, coming forward to read his statement, which at times he struggled to voice through sobs and tears as Brosnahan stood to his right, gently placing a hand on his back at times to urge him on.

"To begin, I would like to thank God, who has protected and sustained me. I would also like to thank the court for giving me this opportunity to accept full responsibility for violating the U.S. sanctions on Afghanistan last year, to express my remorse for what has happened, and to express my gratitude to my family and those who have supported me. I would also like to explain how and why I went to Afghanistan as a soldier with the Taliban in its conflict with the Northern Alliance. First, I want to express my deepest gratitude to my family for their unfaltering love and support. I know they have experienced a tremendous—I know they have experienced a tremendous amount of pain throughout this past year, and for that I am sorry. I would also like to say that I am very grateful to my attorneys, whose support of me has never wavered, to those who treated my wounds on the U.S.S. *Peleliu,* and to those who helped bring me home. I also want to express my appreciation to the many Americans who have supported me and my family through letters, e-mails, and editorials.

"I understand why so many Americans were angry when I was first discovered in Afghanistan. I realize that many still are, but I hope that with time and understanding those feelings will change. I would like to take some time to explain how I ended up in Afghanistan. Prior to May of last year, I was a student of Islam at a school in Pakistan, having previously studied the Arabic language in Yemen. In June, after receiving three weeks of military training in northern Pakistan, I traveled to Afghanistan in order to assist the Taliban government in opposing the warlords of the Northern Alliance. After being required to take additional military training at a facility in Afghanistan, I volunteered as a foot soldier on the front lines in the province of Takhar in northeastern Afghanistan. I arrived there on September 6th, 2001. I went to Afghanistan — I went to Afghanistan because I believed it was my religious duty to assist my fellow Muslims militarily in their jihad against the Northern Alliance.

"Because the term jihad has been commonly misunderstood, I would like to take a few minutes to explain the meaning of the term. In the Arabic language, jihad literally means struggle. In Islamic terminology — in Islamic terminology, jihad refers to the spending of one's utmost exertion in the service of God. I have never understood jihad to mean anti-Americanism or terrorism. I condemn terrorism on every level, unequivocally. My beliefs about jihad are those of mainstream Muslims around the world. I believe that jihad ranges from striving to overcome one's personal faults, to speaking out for the truth in adverse circumstances, to military action in the defense of justice. The type of jihad one practices depends upon one's circumstances, but the essence of any form of jihad lies in the intent. Last year, I felt that I had an obligation to assist what I perceived to be an Islamic liberation movement against the warlords who were occupying several provinces in northern Afghanistan. I had learned from books, articles, and individuals with firsthand experience of numerous atrocities committed by the Northern Alliance against civilians. I had heard reports of massacres—of massacres, child rape, torture, and castration. I also knew that many of these warlords had fought alongside the Soviet Union in the 1980s during the Soviet invasion and occupation of Afghanistan.

"I went to Afghanistan because I believed there was no way to alleviate the suffering of the Afghan people, aside from military action. I did not go to fight against America, and I never did. I saw the war between the Taliban and the Northern Alliance as a continuation of the war between mujaheddin and the Soviets. I knew that the mujaheddin had been supported by the United States. In addition, I knew that the Northern Alliance continued to be funded and armed by the Russian government throughout the 1990s and up until last year.

"My experience of living in Afghanistan was limited to military life, as a trainee and as a soldier. In retrospect, I had no real exposure to the life of civilians under the rule of the Taliban. Since returning to the United States, I have learned more about the Taliban, such as reports—such as reports of the Taliban's repression of women, which I did not see or hear of while I was in Afghanistan, and which I believe is strongly condemned by Islam. I have also become aware of the relationship between the leaders of the Taliban and Osama bin Laden's organization. Bin Laden's terrorist attacks are completely against Islam, completely contrary to the conventions of jihad, and without any justification whatsoever. His grievances, whatever they may be, cannot be addressed by acts of injustice and violence against innocent people in America. Terrorism is never justified, and has proved extremely damaging to Muslims around the world. I have never supported terrorism in any form, and never would. I went to Afghanistan with the intention of fighting against terrorism and oppression, not to support it. Although I thought I knew a good deal about the Taliban when I went to the front line, it is clear to me now that there were many things of which I was not aware.

"I made a mistake by joining the Taliban. I want the court to know, and I want the American people to know, that had I realized then what I know now about the Taliban, I would have never have joined them. When I began my studies in Islam, I had the ambition of one day teaching, writing, and translating Arabic texts into English. I still have these ambitions, and I hope to pursue my studies in Islam, the Arabic language, world history, linguistics, sociology, and English literature. I hope to use this knowledge to serve Islam and the interests of Muslims and around the world to the full extent of my capability. And to conclude, I would like to thank the court again for giving me this opportunity to speak."

All of Lindh's words and emotions rang hollow to the elder Spann as he sat listening. The judge had decided to let Johnny Spann address the court much as a victim of a crime would have the opportunity to speak at a sentencing. Spann's father, technically, by the letter of the plea agreement, was not a victim of Lindh's crimes. Ellis gave Spann the floor anyway, saying it would be callous to refuse him, given the brave sacrifice his son had made in Afghanistan. Shortly after Lindh sat down again, Ellis called up Spann, who stood at the same podium, raw with grief from the recent anniversary of his slain son's departure for Afghanistan.

"I'm sorry to say that I don't believe the things that Mr. Lindh is saying to us," said Spann midway through his remarks, in which he argued that Lindh shared blame for the September 11 attacks because of his association with bin Laden at al-Farooq and raised questions about Lindh's culpability in the death of his son.

"Me, along with thousands and millions of Americans, and millions of people around the world, we saw, as we watched TV, we saw those hijacked airplanes fly into our World Trade Center," Spann went on. "And as I mentioned a while ago, we saw fellow Americans jumping out of the top of those World Trade Centers because they wanted to choose the way they wanted to die. They didn't want to be burned up. Those people that were in the World Trade Center and those people that were in the Pentagon, and those people that was in those airplanes, thought that they were in a safe place. They thought they were going to a safe workplace. They thought they were in the United States of America, and in a safe abode. But we know that it wasn't. And we also know, I think without a doubt I think we all know—and I don't understand, if we don't understand that the al-Qaida members are the ones that flew those airplanes. They are the ones that hijacked them. They came to the United States and they killed our people. So if you are a member of the al-Qaida, whether you are a part of it, whether you actually came and you flew the airplane into the buildings or not, what difference does it make? You are still part of that conspiracy. You trained with them. You learned to fight with them.

"We saw CNN tapes being presented to us over TV. The CNN brought the tapes back from Afghanistan. And we saw how the al-Qaida trained the people in their camps. We saw how they use biological weapons and tested them on animals, and the animals lay there and they kicked until they died. We saw them jumping out of vehicles and off of motorcycles, with their AK-47s and their other weapons, and learning how to kill people. The al-Qaida, in fact, were trained to kill; in fact, trained to kill Americans, with suicide missions, or whatever ways was possible.

"Mr. Lindh, the way I understand it, has admitted that he fought on the front lines of Takhar. Are we supposed to believe that any kind of an army would let somebody come and be a member of their army and be on the front lines, but never fire his weapon? That's a little bit hard for me to believe. And I think it's a little bit hard for the majority of the American people to believe. We know, in fact, that he said he did. We know, in fact, that he went back to Konduz — or I'm sorry, that he retreated back to Konduz. He retreated back to Konduz because he was with the al-Qaida members that were fighting in Takhar. We know that when they surrendered in Konduz, that they were carried down through Mazar-i-Sharif, on trucks, and carried down to Qala-i-Jangi fortress. We also know — I don't think there's a doubt in anybody's mind, we saw it on TV, where John Walker Lindh appeared the next day. So we know that he was in there the night before. We know that he, in fact, spent the night in the pink house, in the pink house that was in the middle of the southern part of the Qala-i-Jangi fortress. And the reports are different, but I am assuming that there were some four hundred plus prisoners in that building.

"Are we to believe that a person could spend the night in a building, that small of a building with four hundred plus prisoners — and a third of them never have been searched, a third of them still have their weapons, they still have their grenades underneath their head gear, underneath their slouchy clothes — are we to believe that those people spent the night there, and they didn't talk about that, 'We've got weapons, we've still got guns?' That's a little hard for me to believe, too, and it's a little hard for the majority of the American people that talked to me to believe. I thought that it was the responsibility of Americans that if you knew that there was something going to happen — and I realize that what you have already said, that evidently the court believes that Mr. Lindh didn't know there was going to be an uprising. It's hard for me to believe that."

"Let me be clear about that," Ellis said, interrupting Spann. "The government has no evidence of that."

"I understand," Spann said.

"And your suspicions, the inferences you draw from the facts are not enough to warrant a jury conviction, even if they are shared by wide segments of the American public," Ellis continued. "But I understand all your suspicions, and I assure you that I had them, too. I assure you that I looked for that evidence. But I share, everyone shares those suspicions."

"I feel like it is not a just punishment," Spann went on. "Some of the things that Mr. Lindh said a while ago about, if he didn't want to fight against Americans, where was he when the uprising started? Did he do anything to help Mike? Did he drag Mike inside the pink house with him? Did he take him anywhere, to try to help him? Did he not know that Mike was an American?"

"Those are all quite legitimate questions," the judge said. "We may not have got it right. But I don't think we—it's an imperfect world. We are not going to know. The only certainty I have about all of it is that I think your son was a hero. That's the only certainty I can see."

CHAPTER TEN

Faith and Silence

AMONG the last of the papers filed in Lindh's case was an essay he wrote as part of a psychological evaluation he underwent in preparation for his aborted trial. The writing was not to be made public, but Ellis, after reading it, felt it should be part of the court record. Lindh agreed. The one-page essay is titled "Thoughts on the Legitimacy of Suicide Bombings." In it, Lindh stressed that he was not an accredited Islamic authority, but nonetheless had some feelings on the matter.

I believe that suicide bombings are not justified regardless of how desperate the conflict may be, or how limited the options of the resisting population. Killing civilians has been unanimously rejected by mainstream Muslim scholars throughout Islamic history.

Those who support the use of suicide bombs compare these acts to the heroic feats of numerous contemporaries of the prophet Mohammed, which he himself praised and encouraged. In battle with the enemies of Islam, Muslim soldiers would hurl themselves toward large groups of enemy combatants, fighting to the death with little or no hope of survival. The key difference is that these fighters were killed by the hands of their enemies; they did not actually take their lives with their own hands. A suicide bomber takes his or her own life along with those attacked, so this is clearly an act of suicide in

187

spite of the fact that such attacks are often very effective from a military standpoint.

A primary motivation of suicide bombers is to achieve martyrdom, which is the desire of every believer in Islam. Martyrdom, however, is a status in the afterlife, which only God can determine. A person cannot "martyr" himself. Even a combatant in a fully justified conflict who, hoping for martyrdom, puts himself in an extremely dangerous situation can only achieve this rank when God chooses to confer it. The belief that a person can achieve martyrdom by committing suicide represents a significant misunderstanding of this principle.

Suicide is explicitly and unconditionally condemned in the Qur'an: "[A]nd do not kill yourselves. Indeed God is most merciful with you." (Qu'ran 4:27.) The prophet Mohammed has clearly explained the gravity of this sin in saying, "Indeed, whoever kills himself will be punished in the fire of hell eternally." [Related by Bukhari (5778) and Muslim (109 & 110) in different forms.] Islam does not accept the idea that the ends justify the means, even in the most desperate and most justified conflicts. "Oh you who believe — stand firmly for God, as witness in justice, and do not let the hatred of people cause you to swerve from that which is right. Be just — that is closer to piety, and fear God; indeed God is well acquainted with what you do." (Qur'an 5:8.)

Ellis had felt that Lindh's writings would help people's understanding of him and his case. But even all that was said at the hearing and in court documents, as well as in the media, didn't answer the questions aired at Lindh's sentencing, questions the judge himself acknowledged were troubling. Lindh left the courtroom that day judged and sentenced, but with those doubts and others still hanging over him.

Was Lindh completely unaware of the Taliban's human rights record as he traveled to Afghanistan, even though the group's gross abuses stood documented publicly for anyone with enough curiosity to do an Internet search? Did Lindh really not understand who bin Laden was and what he stood for when he saw him at al-Farooq, despite the fanatic's fame in both the Western world and the jihadi ranks? Lindh's standing answer to the latter question is one of the more difficult of his claims to believe. Bin Laden has been regarded with cult reverence, particularly in Pakistan and Afghanistan, since the mid 1990s. In Pakistan, his face can be found on countless posters and t-shirts, even notebooks. And his avowed hostility toward the United States was widely understood, even among illiterates in remote places like Bannu. Lindh himself had at least some idea about bin Laden's ideology and politics as far back as 1998, when the Saudi was named by the United States as the organizer of the twin bombings of U.S. embassies in East Africa. Upon his return to the United States from Afghanistan, Lindh claimed to have been unclear about bin Laden's relation to the Taliban, insisting that he thought al-Farooq was a Taliban camp, not a bin Laden camp, even though Arabs, not Afghans, ran things. Yet in his initial interview with Pelton, Lindh offered a clear understanding of exactly what role bin Laden played in funding camps for Arabic speakers in Afghanistan who wanted to fight with the Taliban. Taken altogether, Lindh's stated lack of awareness about whom he was dealing with and what he was doing through the course of his journey reflects a profound measure of ignorance for someone of his obvious intelligence. At best, Lindh was as clueless as he maintains, a trusting, naïve outsider suddenly swept up in a complicated world where his limited education and lack of worldliness left him vulnerable to religious dogma. Perhaps so, but such ignorance would have been a willing blindness on Lindh's part. The slowest Internet connection in Yemen could have tapped Lindh into volumes of credible online news clippings about the Taliban and bin Laden, had he cared to read them. Still, much of what Lindh said in court convinced even some of his harshest critics of his sincerity.

"The tearful statement he made to the court I think was probably the most memorable moment in the case," McNulty said. "It seemed sincere. He really didn't need to put on a show for the judge. It didn't make any difference. The sentence was already determined. So there's no reason why he needed to carry on if he didn't feel that way."

Spann, according to all believable evidence, died in the yard at Qala-i-Jangi, not in the basement with Lindh on hand as his grieving father suspects. A man was killed in that basement while Lindh was present, however. He was an Afghan, an unarmed civilian sent to collect bodies for the Red Cross. Lindh's comrades murdered him, and somewhere loved ones grieve for him without hope of ever seeing the killers face justice where they committed that crime—in Afghanistan. An overriding question in Lindh's case was whether he ever intended to kill Americans in Afghanistan. Lost in that debate was any meaningful recognition of Lindh's obvious intention to fight with a force set on killing Afghans in Afghanistan, an act that would go unjudged in a country with no courts. Lindh refused to be labeled a terrorist in America, where his argument is legitimately debatable legally, morally, and ethically. In Afghanistan, however, the foreigners who fought in northern areas will forever be rightfully remembered as terrorists. Foreign fighters of the sort Lindh joined terrorized northern Afghanistan for years as they fought alongside the Taliban. Lindh followed these men, believing they were just in their cause. At some point along the way, Lindh claims that he became disenchanted when he understood the true nature of the killers he joined. Exactly when Lindh was struck with this epiphany remains unclear, and it's an important question for understanding Lindh, because it directly reflects on his possible culpability in

Spann's death and even the events of September 11. If Lindh indeed understood that bin Laden was a terrorist leader driven to attack civilians in the United States and Israel when he met him, then Lindh was arguably a supporter of al-Qaida, however indirectly, and therefore a party in some way to all the group's bloody aims. Lindh says he didn't realize that bin Laden was a mass murderer inextricably tied to the Taliban. And no witnesses have emerged to challenge Lindh's assertion that he only woke up to the realities of the relationship between the Taliban and bin Laden's terrorist campaign during the final hours of his jihad, after September 11.

Lindh's motivations and thinking from September 11 onward remain perplexing too. By his account, Lindh began to question the morals of jihad in Afghanistan in much the same way he had doubted the cause in Kashmir. If this is true, then Lindh may or may not have had the chance to abandon his Ansar brigade in the weeks after September 11, and he may not have understood all that was happening around him in those days as America entered the war. But it seems impossible that he would not have known people in the basement were armed and plotting a revolt when he sat before Spann, saying nothing that might warn Spann, Tyson, or the Afghans with whom he had struck a peace deal.

I spent several weeks in Afghanistan in the spring of 2002 piecing together what had happened in Konduz and at Qala-i-Jangi, interviewing dozens of witnesses and survivors, even paying a visit to the basement. I also find it hard to believe that Lindh could have spent the hours he did in the cellar before the Qala-i-Jangi uprising and known nothing of the plot that ultimately killed Spann and hundreds of others. The scenario is at first plausible, but ultimately unbelievable: The confined space in the basement left enough room so that, potentially, members of a group at one end could talk among themselves without being overheard by others elsewhere in the hold. Clearly, there were a number of men speaking in Arabic plotting the revolt while Lindh was in the same space. Lindh maintains that he was not speaking with them and, therefore, knew nothing of the planned attack. However, Lindh was speaking with someone in the basement, either in Arabic or English, as evidenced by his claims of overhearing rumors among the prisoners that Dostum's surrender deal still held. It's possible that the Arabic or English speakers with whom Lindh conversed at some point during the night either also knew nothing of the plans or perhaps didn't share the plot with him. Perhaps the prisoners Lindh talked to were part of a group outside the small ring of plotters. But that picture does not reflect the accounts of Enamul Hak and Wahid Ahmad, the two Pakistani Taliban who were also in the basement with Lindh and later remained prisoners of Dostum instead of ending up in Guantanamo Bay. They said the group in the basement was split, with seemingly everyone aware that at least some in their ranks were considering staging an attack. If Hak and Ahmad are to be believed, then Lindh knew of the revolt, a foresight that would make him culpable in Spann's death. However, the judge in Lindh's case had access to reports of interrogations from other witnesses to events at Qala-i-Jangi being held incommunicado in Cuba. Those reports, apparently, showed no link between Lindh and the uprising's plotters, as the judge stressed.

Ultimately, it's impossible to tell what Lindh heard or didn't hear in the basement that night and what he knew as he sat before Spann. But if Lindh was still unclear on any matters about Ansar, the Taliban, or bin Laden at that point, Spann spelled it all out for him—and offered to help him leave. Spann told Lindh in those haunting moments the two Americans shared that "the people here you're working with are terrorists." In that instant Lindh held in his mind everything he needed to understand the mistake he had made in joining the Taliban; he had his own growing doubts about the Taliban, Ansar, and bin Laden, plus an increasing awareness of the sickening carnage of September 11. More importantly, Spann offered Lindh a way out, right then. There, in that second, Lindh made a choice, a decision that said more about his nature than any statement ever could, in my opinion. He chose to stay with bin Laden's trained killers. And initially, he showed no regrets. In Lindh's one interview, Pelton asked him if Afghanistan had been the right cause in the right place. Lindh told him, "It is exactly what I thought it would be." There is, of course, Lindh's tearful statement of remorse in court to remember. Like others, I found Lindh's words believably heartfelt, but nonetheless somehow vain given that they came only after his family and his lawyers explained again what he already knew when he wordlessly turned away from Spann.

All the recriminations, unanswered questions, and lingering suspicions don't trouble Lindh, who was serving out days at the Alexandria jail through the early weeks of 2003, while waiting to be transferred to a facility closer to his family.

"He's peaceful, at peace with himself," said Abdelwahab Hassan, a volunteer prison counselor for Muslim inmates at the Alexandria Detention Center, who got to know Lindh over the course of 2002. An Egyptian-born American, Hassan spent about twenty minutes each week with Lindh, talking to him through the food slot of the door to his cell, where Lindh spent his days alone in a space about the size of a walk-in closet.

"We read the Koran and we interpret some of the Koran," said Hassan, who lives near the jail and has done prison counseling there since 1999. "I started talking with him in Arabic," Hassan said. "He wants to remember the Arabic."

Lindh had requested a Muslim counselor when he first arrived at the Alexandria jail, and Hassan, after undergoing a government security check, was allowed to include Lindh in his weekly rounds. Hassan had heard about Lindh even before the American wound up an inmate in Alexandria. Hassan had even printed up Internet articles about Lindh around the time Lindh was first captured and followed the story closely in the news. "It was an interesting story to me, someone who is American, who traveled half of the world for Islam," said Hassan, a middle-aged man with a calm, clean-shaven face and mellow voice, slightly accented.

When Lindh arrived in Virginia, Hassan was somewhat concerned that the captured fighter might hold unorthodox views on Islam because of his jihadi experience. In their first meetings, Hassan tried to get a feel for Lindh's religious leanings, listening closely for anything in Lindh's Islamic beliefs that sounded radical. "He seemed to be accepting of all I said," Hassan said. "There was nothing strange."

Lindh, Hassan learned, was a garden variety Muslim, a believer with a faith no different than the roughly one billion followers of Islam worldwide. Lindh, by Hassan's assessment, does not adhere to the conservative Wahhabism or Salafi thought. He is not militant or fanatic. He is simply a Sunni with everyday, mainstream views on Islam.

Lindh, of course, differs in some important ways from most Muslim prisoners Hassan has gotten to know at the jail. Most are poor minorities who have converted to Islam, none of whom hold Lindh's kind of notoriety.

"Sometimes he thinks his case is exaggerated because of the political situation," Hassan said. "He's not the only American who went to Afghanistan. There were many, many people, many Americans, who went to Afghanistan and fought with the Taliban, and their cases didn't take this popularity."

Lindh didn't dwell on his case, though, at least not with Hassan. Mostly the two talked about religious matters, how the

Koran can be applied to everyday life. And they talked about books; Lindh kept many in his cell and pulled regularly from the Alexandria prison library. In addition, Hassan gave Lindh a number of readings in Arabic, including a volume on the Islamic meaning of patience. Hassan thought it would help ease the years ahead.

"All that he wants is to lead a life that pleases God," Hassan said of Lindh. "John is not an evil person. He's a very nice person. He has nothing in his heart against America. He has nothing in his heart against anyone in America. He does not wish any harm to anyone in America, unlike what some people think. He's an American, and he's proud to be American. But he is proud more of being Muslim. He's proud more to belonging to his creator. He thinks his creator is more important than America."

Lindh's American name still didn't quite fit, apparently, and neither did any of the names he carried during his journey. Lindh told Hassan that he was considering yet another Islamic moniker for himself. Lindh was thinking of going by Hamzah, the name of one of the prophet Mohammed's uncles. It's an interesting choice. Hamzah, by all accounts, was one of Mohammed's bravest fighters, a man of enormous strength and legendary bravery who ultimately died a martyr's death. "He's a courageous man that the prophet praised and he has a very interesting biography, Hamzah," Hassan said. "He was strong, strong in his belief and strong in his character."

I asked Hassan why Lindh changed his name so often. Lindh had never explained the reason to Hassan, who could only guess. "He's still in the process of choosing the real name that he wants to be."

Epilogue

ON JANUARY 25, 2003, a Saturday, John Phillip Walker Lindh traveled. Under guard by federal marshals, Lindh flew across the country from the Alexandria Detention Center he had called home for a year to the Federal Correctional Institution in Victorville, California, a former airbase turned into a medium-security prison sitting in the desert eighty-four miles northeast of Los Angeles. There, Lindh joined about sixteen hundred other double-bunked inmates, who typically spend days doing prison chores like laundry, cooking, and groundskeeping. The cell Lindh shares with another inmate has a window, and sometimes Lindh is allowed to mix with the other prisoners, about twenty of whom are fellow Muslims born in the United States. Lindh busies himself in Victorville much as he did in Alexandria, spending hours translating Arabic texts and reading newspapers, as well as books ranging from Viktor Frankl's *Man's Search for Meaning* to the Harry Potter novels.

The final leg of Lindh's voyage hardly made the news. The Associated Press wrote of Lindh's transfer in less than three hundred words with a story that appeared five days afterward. Lindh's arrival in California was something of a local story around Los Angeles, briefly. Other than that, few seemed to care.

The quiet trip and lack of media interest suits Lindh, who hopes to fade altogether from the news—and popular consciousness. Lindh was always embarrassed by the attention given to him, and he told attorney George Harris once that it seemed as though every effort made to tell his story in the media by his family and legal team appeared only to further misconceptions about him and his religion. Better to let the world forget, Lindh told Harris, than try to make them understand.

Lindh is worth thinking about every now and again, though, even if we never hear from him. For Lindh unwittingly showed us some truths about widespread feelings among many Muslims towards the United States, animosities shaped by America's own actions.

Unlike others who answered calls to Islamic holy wars, Lindh's motivations for jihad were not colored by years spent in the desperate squalor of Arab slums or refugee camps, like many foreigners who traveled to Afghanistan. He was not an angry outsider living as a poor minority on the fringes of Western societies, such as the accused twentieth hijacker Zacarias Moussaoui from France or Richard Reid, the sworn al-Qaida follower from Britain, who tried to down an airliner mid-flight with a bomb in his shoe. Raised in a fine American suburb, Lindh was a shy, thoughtful individual with a spiritual side, not a warped personality. And yet this rather average young man, while exploring his newfound religion, began to identify in some ways with the same feelings that drive the madman terrorizing our world today. And if a quiet kid from Marin County can relate to the underlying ideals of such a cause, then perhaps anyone can.

Take a walk through a Palestinian refugee camp, or talk long enough to someone who's been there, and you too might see why so many view U.S. support for Israel as akin to an American backing of apartheid South Africa. Hear stories about Russian atrocities in Chechnya, and you might understand why the guerrilla insurgency there is so lasting, despite years of military efforts by Russia, now counted among America's closer allies.

Lindh heard these stories and more, absorbing hatreds little understood by those living in American society. Through travels and religious exploration, Lindh opened himself to a realm of millions who can claim, with varying legitimacy, to be victims of the United States and its actions on the world stage. And while Lindh held many misconceptions, the empathy he shared with other jihadis of his age was rooted in real injustices. As an obvious example, the weaponry most often used by Israeli forces that repeatedly leads to civilian casualties in Palestinian territories is American made. This fact is not lost on Palestinians and their sympathizers, who include world leaders of stature, terrorist maniacs, and everyday Muslims like Lindh.

Palestine wasn't Lindh's cause for a number of reasons, but the modern Islamic ethos of jihad that Lindh took to heart is a legacy of the conflict between Palestinians and Israelis. Nearly ceaseless fighting in the Middle East for more than fifty years has radicalized scores of men like Lindh's ghost mentor Shaykh Abdullah Azzam throughout the region, where the United States has had a hand in the wars. The rise of Islamic militancy throughout the world, in all of the regional variations Lindh struggled to understand, echoes the violence in the Middle East. Just ask any Arab you find in Afghanistan, Kashmir, Chechnya, or elsewhere. Witness Lindh.

Indeed, it's difficult to imagine that militant Islamists like Osama bin Laden or Shaykh Abdullah Azzam would have emerged from the Middle East as fighters driven to undertake global campaigns with the help of idealistic young men like Lindh if Arab lands had been at peace in past generations. But the decades of bloodletting, which the United States and its allies at times have abetted, further sickened the tortured minds of men the United States called allies once in Afghanistan, but today names as enemies.

None of this is to say that the United States is to blame for the sad state of Afghanistan, the inability of the Palestinians and Israelis to live in peace, the carnage in Chechnya, the strife in Kashmir, or the many ills plaguing other Muslim lands where America has interests. Such troubled regions, as Lindh came to understand too late, are in the grips of historical problems that go deeper than any one nation can create or resolve. But the United States would be wise as a country to better understand the implications of its actions in the Islamic world, because looking back over recent history, we can see the steps we took into the conflict we now find ourselves. Lindh confusingly stumbled through some of these pasts in his strange journey. And I've come to think that, along the way, he unconsciously marked some of the wrong moves America made in its dealings with the Muslim world—the backing of Islamic militants against the Soviet Union, the inequitable policy regarding the Palestinian-Israeli conflict, the support of corrupt Middle Eastern regimes for economic and geopolitical gains. The missteps are worth examining so that the United States may work to reverse them, as well as avoid a similar path in our ongoing affairs in the Islamic world, which will deepen profoundly and irreversibly in the coming years. Lindh, while his story drops from the news and falls into a far corner of our minds as he sits in prison, offers a living reminder still that America risks creating as many enemies as it destroys among Muslims unless it acts now and in the future with greater moral clarity.

Selected Bibliography

Armstrong, Karen. *Islam: A Short History*. London: Weidenfeld and Nicolson, 2000.

Armstrong, Karen. *Muhammad: A Biography of the Prophet*. U.K.: Victor Gollancz, Ltd., 1991.

Ahmed, Salahuddin. *A Dictionary of Muslim Names*. London: C. Hurst and Co., 1999.

Ali, Maulana Muhammad. *A Manual of Hadith*. Lahore: Ahmadiyya Association for the Propagation of Islam, 1941.

Azzam, Sheykh Abdullah. *Defense of the Muslim Lands*. London: Azzam Publications, 1996.

Azzam, Sheykh Abdullah. *Join the Caravan*. London: Azzam Publications, 1996.

Bakhtiar, Laleh. *Encyclopedia of Islamic Law: A Compendium of the Major Schools*. Chicago: ABC International Group, Inc., 1996.

Cooley, John K. *Unholy Wars, Afghanistan, America and International Terrorism*. London: Pluto Press, 2001.

Dresch, Paul. *A History of Modern Yemen*. Cambridge, U.K.: Cambridge University Press, 2001.

Dupree, Nancy Hatch. *A Historical Guide to Afghanistan*. Kabul: Afghan Tourist Organization, 1970.

Esposito, John L. (ed.). *The Oxford Encyclopedia of the Modern Islamic World*. Oxford, U.K.: Oxford University Press, 1995.

Ewans, Martin. *Afghanistan, A New History*. Richmond, U.K.: Curzon Press, 2001.

Ganguly, Sumit. *Conflict Unending: India-Pakistan Tensions Since 1947*. New York: Columbia University Press, 2001.

Goldziher, Ignaz. *Introduction to Islamic Theology and Law.* Trans. Andras and Ruth Hamori. Princeton: Princeton Univiersity Press, 1981.

Griffin, Michael. *Reaping the Whirlwind: The Taliban Movement in Afghanistan.* London: Pluto Press, 2001.

Hallaq, Wael B. *A History of Islamic Legal Theories.* Cambridge, U.K.: Cambridge University Press, 1997.

Hedges, Chris. *War Is a Force That Gives Us Meaning.* New York: Public Affairs, 2002.

Hopkirk, Peter. *The Great Game.* London: John Murray, 1970.

Kaplan, Robert D. *Soldiers of God: With Islamic Warriors in Afghanistan and Pakistan.* New York: Vintage Books, 1990.

Mackintosh-Smith, Tim. *Yemen: The Unknown Arabia.* New York: Overlook Press, 2001.

Marsden, Peter. *The Taliban: War and Religion in Afghanistan.* London: Zed Books, 2002.

Pelton, Robert Young. *The World's Most Dangerous Places.* 4th ed. New York: HarperCollins, 2000.

Rais, Rasul Bakhsh. *War without Winners: Afghanistan's Uncertain Transition after the Cold War.* Oxford, U.K.: Oxford University Press, 1997.

Rashid, Ahmed. *Taliban, Militant Islam, Oil and Fundamentalism in Central Asia.* New Haven: Yale University Press, 2001.

X, Malcolm, and Alex Haley. *The Autobiography of Malcolm X.* New York: Ballantine Books, 1973.

MEDIA SOURCES

Associated Press, Agence France Press, *Time Magazine, Newsweek, U.S. News & World Report, The New Yorker, The Atlantic Monthly, New York Times, Washington Post, Wall Street Journal, Los Angeles Times, San Francisco Chronicle, Baltimore Sun, Christian Science Monitor,* Cable News Network, National Public Radio.

About the Author

MARK KUKIS left a job as a White House correspondent for United Press International shortly after September 11, 2001, to cover the war in Afghanistan as a freelance writer. Beginning in October of that year, Kukis spent several months in Pakistan and Afghanistan covering the conflict, including stays in Jalalabad and Tora Bora to report on fighting there for the online magazine salon.com. Kukis graduated with a bachelor's degree in journalism from the University of Texas, Austin, in 1998, the same year he served as an election monitor in Bosnia, before settling in Washington, D.C., to pursue writing. He lives in Washington, D.C.